MW01504243

Witness Lee

A Deeper Study
of the
DIVINE
DISPENSING

Living Stream Ministry
Anaheim, California • www.lsm.org

First Edition, December 1990.

ISBN 978-0-87083-562-9

Published by

Living Stream Ministry
2431 W. La Palma Ave., Anaheim, CA 92801 U.S.A.
P. O. Box 2121, Anaheim, CA 92814 U.S.A.

Printed in the United States of America

12   13   14   15   16   17   /   11   10   9   8   7   6   5

CONTENTS

Section III

The Divine Dispensing of the All-inclusive Christ and Its Functions

Section IV

The Divine Dispensing of the Divine Trinity and the Producing and Building Up of the Church

PREFACE

This book is composed of translated messages given by Brother Witness Lee in the conferences in Malaysia from October 23 to November 7, 1990. Chapters one and two contain messages given in Kota Kinabulu on the divine dispensing as seen from the Gospel of John. Chapters three to seven with the two supplementary words comprise the messages given in Sibu on the divine dispensing as seen from the book of Romans. Chapters eight to ten are composed of messages given in Kuching on the divine dispensing as seen from 1 and 2 Corinthians. Chapters eleven to fifteen comprise the messages given in Petaling Jaya on the divine dispensing as seen from Ephesians. The original messages were given in Chinese.

The outline and the Scripture reading at the beginning of each chapter are meant to be used as a help for saints to share the riches in each chapter corporately in meetings of mutuality.

SECTION I

The Divine Dispensing of the Divine Trinity
and Its Results

CHAPTER ONE

THE ACCOMPLISHMENT OF THE DIVINE DISPENSING OF THE DIVINE TRINITY

OUTLINE AND SCRIPTURE READING

I. The Divine Trinity—the Father, the Son, and the Spirit:

A. The Father expressed in the Son—the Son being the embodiment of the Father—John 14:8-11.

John 14:8-11
Philip said to Him, Lord, show us the Father and it suffices us. (9) Jesus said to him, Am I so long a time with you, and you have not known Me, Philip? He who has seen Me has seen the Father. How is it that you say, Show us the Father? (10) Do you not believe that I am in the Father, and the Father is in Me? The words which I speak to you, I do not speak from Myself; but the Father who abides in Me, He does His works. (11) Believe Me that I am in the Father and the Father in Me; but if not, believe Me because of the works themselves.

B. The Son realized as the Spirit—the Spirit being the reality of the Son—John 14:16-20.

John 14:16-20
And I will ask the Father, and He will give you another Comforter, that He may be with you forever; (17) even the Spirit of reality, whom the world cannot receive, because it does not

behold Him or know Him; but you know Him, because He abides with you and shall be in you. (18) I will not leave you orphans; I am coming to you. (19) Yet a little while and the world beholds Me no longer, but you behold Me; because I live, you shall live also. (20) In that day you shall know that I am in My Father, and you in Me, and I in you.

II. The accomplishment of the divine dispensing of the Divine Trinity:

A. The Triune God becoming the flesh, dispensing Himself as grace and reality to man—John 1:1, 14, 16.

John 1:1

In the beginning was the Word, and the Word was with God, and the Word was God.

John 1:14

And the Word became flesh and tabernacled among us...full of grace and reality.

John 1:16

For of His fullness we all received, and grace upon grace.

B. The Triune God dispensing the Son as eternal life to His believers—John 3:16.

John 3:16

For God so loved the world that He gave His only begotten Son, that everyone who believes in Him should not perish, but have eternal life.

C. The Son dying to release the divine life and to dispense it to all the members of His Body—John 12:24.

John 12:24

Truly, truly, I say to you, unless a grain of wheat falls into the ground and dies, it abides alone; but if it dies, it bears much fruit.

D. **The Son resurrecting to be transfigured as the Spirit to be the ultimate consummation of the Triune God, that the Triune God may be dispensed into the believers—John 20:8-9, 19, 22.**

John 20:8-9

Then therefore the other disciple also, who came first to the tomb, entered, and he saw and believed. (9) For as yet they did not know the Scripture, that He must rise from among the dead.

John 20:19

When therefore it was evening on that day, the first day of the week, and when the doors were shut where the disciples were for fear of the Jews, Jesus came and stood in the midst and said to them, Peace be to you.

John 20:22

And when He had said this, He breathed into them and said to them, Receive the Holy Spirit.

E. **The Son being above all, inheriting all, and being sent from God to speak God's word, and dispensing the Spirit without measure— John 3:31-36.**

John 3:31-36

He who comes from above is above all; he who is of the earth is of the earth and speaks of the earth. He who comes from heaven is above all. (32) What He has seen and heard, of this He testifies, and no one receives His testimony. (33) He who receives His testimony has sealed that God is true. (34) For He whom God has sent speaks the words of God, for He gives the Spirit not by measure. (35) The Father loves the Son, and has given all into His hand. (36) He

who believes in the Son has eternal life; but
he who disobeys the Son shall not see life, but
the wrath of God abides on him.

THE DIVINE ECONOMY

Thank the Lord that we can have this conference. In this conference the Lord has given me a burden to consider with you the divine dispensing of the Divine Trinity and its result. First, we will consider the accomplishment of the divine dispensing of the Divine Trinity.

The divine dispensing of the Divine Trinity is a great matter. It is something that God has planned, purposed, and arranged. In eternity past, God had a divine economy. Based on this economy, He had a move to accomplish His divine dispensing. The first thing that God accomplished is the creation of all things. In His creation, there are the heavens, the earth, and the myriads of created things. But among all these things man is the center. In Genesis 1, we see that God spent only a few days to create all things. After all things were ready, on the last day He created man. When man came out of God's creating hands, he had no lack. He had everything he needed for his eating, dwelling, working, and living. At that time, God did not reveal to any of His creatures, not even to the angels, the purpose of His creating all things, including the heavens, the earth, and man. This mystery of the creation was hidden in Himself.

After God created all the other things, He created man. He created man with a distinctive feature: man was created according to His own image. In other words, He created man according to what He is. God's image, that is, what He is, is that which is in God, which is love, light, holiness, and righteousness. He is love, He is light, He is holiness, and He is righteousness. God created man according to this love, light, holiness, and righteousness. For this reason, there are these four virtues within man. Although we have become fallen because of our ancestor Adam, and have been damaged and have become corrupted, within every one of us there is still love and light. We still prefer holiness to being common, and we all want to be righteous and do not want to make mistakes or to wrong others. The reason for this is that we are all created according to the image of God. Man is like God.

Moreover, God created man after His outward likeness.

Although, on the one hand, the Bible says that God is invisible, yet, on the other hand, God created man according to His image and after His likeness. Hence, man is the most comely object among all of God's creatures. I believe every one of us appreciates himself when he looks in the mirror. The more we look at ourselves the more we like ourselves, because we are made according to God. Genesis 1 says that God created all things after their kind. Man was created according to God. Hence, man is of God's kind. We are of God's kind, because we are created according to God. This is like your picture being made according to you. Although it does not have your life and nature, it is truly your portrait. Of course, it is equally right to say that this picture is not you, because you have a life, nature, and thoughts; you can breathe and speak, whereas the picture cannot do any of these things. From this we can see the relationship between God and us. God is the source of man, and man is the expression of God.

In eternity past, God had an eternal plan, which is to work Himself into a group of chosen people. For this reason, He created man, not only according to His image, but with a spirit, so that man can receive Him and express Him. The man that God created has a spirit, a soul, and a body. We need not probe into the spirit and the soul. The outward body alone is wonderful enough to confound the mind of the best doctors. In addition to this body, there is also the soul, with its thoughts, loves, and concepts. How wonderful it is! Only after we have understood the Bible a little will we understand ourselves, for it is the Bible that has unveiled to us God's revelation. It tells us that God created man according to His image with the purpose that He would enter into the created man. Since we are created according to Him, it becomes comfortable and good for Him to enter into us. If we live in a rented house, we will not feel entirely comfortable while living in it, because the house was not built according to our intention. My house in Anaheim was built for me by the brothers. I am not a civil engineer, nor do I know anything about architecture. But I did know how the house was to be built. I drew up a plan according to my own intention. After the brothers finished building it, I moved in and indeed felt comfortable in it. This is because it was built according to my intention and my plan. The same is true with God. He had a desire, which is that one day He would move in and dwell in the man He created.

However, the man God created fell. But God would not give up. He came personally to accomplish redemption and to fulfill His purpose. We who are created by God are God's vessels, and we are made to contain God. If there are still friends among us tonight who have not believed in the Lord, I would tell you respectfully that belief in God is the greatest truth. Because we are vessels created by God, we will feel empty if we do not have God within. Whenever God comes in, we feel that we are on solid ground. Every one among us, whether old or young, can testify of this. Before we believed in the Lord, we were empty within. There was no content, and our feet were not on solid ground. One day, we heard the gospel and called on the name of the Lord Jesus. He entered into us to be our life, and He has become our content.

God's goal is not merely to have many individual believers. He wants to have a corporate man, who is the church, as His counterpart, His Body, for His corporate expression. This is God's eternal economy, His plan, His purpose, and His arrangement. It is also the desire of God's heart. This matter is clearly revealed in the Bible.

After I was saved I began to love the Bible very much. This book has been in my hands for sixty-five years. I read it nearly every day. The way it is written is very wonderful. Concerning any subject, the way it is revealed to us is a little here and a little there. When I read it, I was like a child playing with a jigsaw puzzle. I have been playing with this puzzle for many years. Now the Bible has become a clear picture within me. It shows us that in eternity past, God had a desire, which is to gain a group of people the same as He is, so that He can enter into them to be their life, their nature and everything to them. In the end, He is not only joined to these people, but is mingled with them as one. These people become His believers, and He gathers them together in His life in various localities to be the churches in those places. These churches constitute the Body of Christ, which is His corporate expression. We are now in such a process.

THE DIVINE DISPENSING

My burden in this conference is to fellowship with you concerning the divine dispensing of the Divine Trinity. God is one, yet He has a distinction of three. The purpose of the Divine Trinity is to work Himself into His created man. Because He wants to enter into us, He has to be triune. He must be the Father, the Son, and the Spirit, at the same time being one entity.

In the Bible, the book that speaks most thoroughly and clearly concerning God being triune is the Gospel of John.

Forty or more years ago, when I first went to Taiwan, a friend of mine once sent me a big watermelon. When my children saw it, they were very happy. They asked what should be done to it. I took the melon to the kitchen, cut it into pieces, and pressed it into juice. Then I gave the drink to the children. In the end, the melon became part of the children's constitution. Hence, in order that the whole melon could enter into the children through their little mouths, it had to pass through this process.

In the same way, our God is triune for the purpose of working Himself into us. He is the Father, the whole melon. He is also the Son, being cut into pieces. He is also the Spirit, being pressed into juice. In order for a big melon to enter into man, it must pass through all these processes. These steps are the stages of the dispensing. Not only does the melon need to be dispensed, but it must also be digested and assimilated into the constitution of man. In the same way, the Triune God—the Father, the Son, and the Spirit—has been processed to become the life-giving Spirit so that we can drink Him and so that He can become our element. This is the divine dispensing of the Divine Trinity.

THE DIVINE TRINITY—
THE FATHER, THE SON, AND THE SPIRIT

The Father Expressed in the Son—
the Son Being the Embodiment of the Father

The Gospel of John speaks of the truth concerning the Triune God in a most profound way. First, it shows us that the Father is expressed in the Son. In other words, the Son is the embodiment of the Father. In John 14, one of the Lord's disciples, Philip, said to the Lord, "Lord, show us the Father and it suffices us." Jesus said to him, "Am I so long a time with you, and you have not known Me, Philip? He who has seen Me has seen the Father...The words which I speak to you, I do not speak from Myself; but the Father who abides in Me, He does His works. Believe Me that I am in the Father and the Father in Me" (vv. 8-11). Hence, the Son is the embodiment of the Father, and He expresses the Father among the disciples. The Son came in the name of the Father and worked in the name of the Father (John 5:43; 10:25). This means that He and the Father are one (John 10:30). He lives because of the Father (John 6:57), and the Father works in Him.

The Son Realized as the Spirit—
the Spirit Being the Reality of the Son

Following this, the Lord said again in John 14:16-20, "And I will ask the Father, and He will give you another Comforter, that He may be with you forever; even the Spirit of reality...He abides with you and shall be in you. I will not leave you orphans; I am coming to you...because I live, you shall live also. In that day you shall know that I am in My Father, and you in Me, and I in you." This shows us that the Son is the embodiment and the expression of the Father, and that the Spirit is the reality and the realization of the Son. The Father in the Son is expressed among the believers, and the Son becoming the Spirit is realized in the believers. Hence, the Father is in the Son, and the Son becomes the Spirit. The Triune God has dispensed Himself into us to become our portion, so that we can enjoy Him as our everything in the Divine Trinity.

THE ACCOMPLISHMENT OF THE DIVINE DISPENSING
OF THE DIVINE TRINITY

The Triune God Becoming the Flesh,
Dispensing Himself as Grace and Reality to Man

Before the Triune God became flesh, the divine dispensing

was not yet realized. It was not until four thousand years after creation that Christ was born to be a man. This was the first step of God's dispensing into man. John 1 shows us that the Word who was God from the beginning became flesh and came among men, full of grace and reality (John 1:1, 14). For the Word to become flesh was for the Triune God to become a man of flesh. In this way, God entered into the sinful man and was joined as one with the sinful man. But He had only the form of the sinful man; He did not have the sin of the sinful man. This can be seen from the type of the brass serpent lifted up by Moses in the wilderness (John 3:14). In this way, He became a sinless God-man. This God-man is the complete God and a perfect man, having both divinity and humanity. He is the One prophesied in Isaiah 9:6, "For unto us a child is born, unto us a son is given...and his name shall be called...the mighty God, the everlasting Father." He is the child, yet He is God. He is the Son, yet He is also the Father. He is the mysterious God-man.

Moreover, all those who believe in Him have also become God-men. John 1:12-13 says, "But as many as received Him, to them He gave authority to become children of God, to those who believe in His name: who were born...of God." Those who were born of man are men. Hence, those who were born of God are gods. But this does not mean that we who are born of God share in His Godhead. We do not have God's person, and we cannot be worshiped as God. However, as far as our life goes, we are the same as God is. God has regenerated us and has given His life to us. This is like being begotten of our father; we share the same life as our father. He is a man. As those begotten of him, we are also men. However, we do not have the position of the father. From this point of view, we are the same as the God who has regenerated us, and He and we are both God-men.

When the Triune God became flesh, He dispensed Himself to men as grace and reality. This grace is God enjoyed by man, and this reality is God gained by man. In John 4, the Lord Jesus went purposely to Sychar in Samaria and sat by the well of Jacob, waiting for a Samaritan woman to come to draw water. The Lord Jesus told her, "If you knew the gift of God, and who it is that says to you, Give Me a drink, you would have asked Him, and He would have given you living water." Then He said, "But whoever drinks of the water that I shall give him shall by no means thirst forever" (vv. 10, 14). The Lord Jesus freely gave the living water to man. There is no price to be paid and no labor required. This is grace. Furthermore, this living water can give man the satisfaction of life and can quench man's deepest thirst. This is reality. This living water is the Triune God, the Father, the Son, and the Spirit, with the Father expressed in the Son, and the Son realized as the Spirit, being dispensed into man. In John 7 the Lord Jesus also said, "If anyone thirst, let him come to Me and drink. He who believes in Me...out of his innermost being shall flow rivers of living water." The Lord Jesus said this concerning the Spirit, whom those who believed in Him were about to receive (John 7:37-39). The Spirit is the consummation of the Triune God. He is the living water, given to us freely. This is grace. When we receive Him, our thirst is satisfied, and we are no longer empty. This is reality.

In John 9 we see a man born blind. The Lord Jesus as the light of the world came to him, spat on the ground, made clay of the spittle, anointed his eyes with the clay, and ordered him to wash in the pool of Siloam. When he washed, he came back seeing (John 9:1-7). He did not pay any price, yet he was healed freely. This is God's grace. The Lord Jesus as the light of the world had caused him to see and to be no longer blind. This is reality.

The Triune God Dispensing the Son as Eternal Life to His Believers

The Son as God's grace and reality is dispensed into all those who believe in Him. In other words, as the eternal life, God's only begotten Son is dispensed to us (John 3:16).

The Son Dying to Release the Divine Life and to Dispense It to All the Members of His Body

John 12:24 shows us that the Lord Jesus as the divine grain of wheat—containing the divine life and glory—released the divine life through the breaking of the shell of His body in death to produce many grains to be formed into one loaf, which is the church, the Body of Christ, to be His increase, for the expression of His glory. This is the divine dispensing.

The Son Resurrecting to Be Transfigured as the Spirit to Be the Ultimate Consummation of the Triune God, That the Triune God May Be Dispensed into the Believers

When the Lord entered into resurrection, He became the life-giving Spirit. The Word which was there in the beginning was the Triune God Himself. He became flesh, passed through human living, crucifixion, resurrection, and ultimately, in resurrection became the Spirit, who is the ultimate consummation of the Triune God.

On the night of resurrection, the Lord came into the midst of the disciples and breathed into them a breath, saying, "Receive the Holy Spirit" (John 20:22). The Holy Spirit here is actually the resurrected Christ Himself, because the Spirit is simply His breath. The Word which was there in the beginning eventually became the breath, who is the Triune God Himself. The Father is the source, the Son is the flow, and the Spirit is the realization. The Triune God is realized as the life-giving Spirit. This is like the big watermelon becoming the melon juice that has become easy for man to receive. Hence, 1 Corinthians 12:13 says, "we were...all given to drink one Spirit." By this, the Triune God Himself is dispensed into us to be our life and everything to us. This is the accomplishment of the divine dispensing of the Divine Trinity.

The Son Being above All, Inheriting All, and Being Sent from God to Speak God's Word, and Dispensing the Spirit without Measure

John 3 reveals to us that this Son who became flesh, died, and resurrected to become the Spirit, is above all, inheriting all, and is sent from God to speak God's word. In the Old Testament time, God spoke through the prophets. But in the New Testament, He speaks to us in the Son (Heb. 1:1-2a). The Son is simply God Himself. He is the expressed God.

While He was on earth, whatever He spoke, whether it was teaching, preaching of the gospel, or discourses, and whether it was spoken on the mountain, by the seashore, or in the houses, it was all the Father's words.

According to the principle of the Bible, the word of God is simply God Himself. To hear God's word is to hear God. To receive God's word is to receive God. Moreover, the word and the Spirit cannot be separated from each other. The word is the Spirit (John 6:63). While the Lord Jesus was on earth, not only did He speak for God, but He also came to dispense the Spirit (John 3:34). The Spirit is the ultimate consummation of the Triune God. Through this dispensing which is without measure, the processed Triune God is injected into us to become our all.

The Spirit is not merely the Spirit of God before the Lord's incarnation. It is the Spirit of God after the Lord's resurrection. As such, He is the mingling of the Holy Spirit, bearing the divine nature, with the Lord's incarnation (His humanity), human living, crucifixion, and resurrection. This is typified by the holy ointment that was produced by olive oil mingled with four spices, as described in Exodus 30:23-25. In this compound Spirit, there is divinity, humanity, the effectiveness of Christ's death, and the fragrance of His resurrection. This Spirit is God; He is the Father and the Son, and Jesus Christ. When we call on the name of the Lord, He enters into us, and He is joined to us and mingled with us, dispensing into us Himself together with all His riches, to be our life and life supply.

Today, to be a genuine Christian who loves the Lord, we do not need to pursue after other things. We only need to grow and to advance day by day in this mingling of God with man. By this, we will grow with the growth of God (Col. 2:19).

(A message given by Brother Witness Lee in Kota Kinabulu, Malaysia on October 24, 1990)

CHAPTER TWO

THE BELIEVERS' ENJOYMENT AND APPLICATION OF THE DIVINE DISPENSING OF THE DIVINE TRINITY AND ITS RESULTS

OUTLINE AND SCRIPTURE READING

I. The believers' enjoyment and application of the divine dispensing of the Divine Trinity:

   A. Regenerated to receive God's Spirit of life, begetting into the believers' spirit that which is the life of Christ—John 3:3-6.

   John 3:3-6
   Jesus answered and said to him, Truly, truly, I say to you, unless a man is born anew, he cannot see the kingdom of God. (4) Nicodemus said to Him, How can a man be born when he is old? He cannot enter the second time into his mother's womb and be born, can he? (5) Jesus answered, Truly, truly, I say to you, unless a man is born of water and the Spirit, he cannot enter into the kingdom of God. (6) That which is born of the flesh is flesh, and that which is born of the Spirit is spirit.

   B. Breathing the pneumatic Christ as breath— John 20:22.

   John 20:22
   And when He had said this, He breathed into them and said to them, Receive the Holy Spirit.

   C. Drinking the pneumatic Christ as the living water—John 4:10, 14; 7:37-39.

John 4:10

Jesus answered and said to her, If you knew the gift of God, and who it is that says to you, Give Me a drink, you would have asked Him, and He would have given you living water.

John 4:14

But whoever drinks of the water that I shall give him shall by no means thirst forever; but the water that I shall give him shall become in him a spring of water welling up into eternal life.

John 7:37-39

Now on the last day, the great day of the feast, Jesus stood and cried out, saying, If anyone thirst, let him come to Me and drink. (38) He who believes in Me, as the Scripture said, out of his innermost being shall flow rivers of living water. (39) But this He said concerning the Spirit, whom those who believed in Him were about to receive; for the Spirit was not yet, because Jesus was not yet glorified.

D. **Eating the Christ who is in the living word of life as the spiritual food—John 6:48, 57b-58a, 63.**

John 6:48

I am the bread of life.

John 6:57b-58a

...so he who eats Me shall also live because of Me. (58a) This is the bread which came down out of heaven...

John 6:63

It is the Spirit who gives life; the flesh profits nothing; the words which I have spoken unto you are spirit and are life.

E. **Growing in the bountiful supply of Christ as the true vine—John 15:1, 4-5.**

John 15:1
I am the true vine, and My Father is the husbandman.

John 15:4-5
Abide in Me and I in you. As the branch cannot bear fruit of itself unless it abides in the vine, so neither can you, unless you abide in Me. (5) I am the vine, you are the branches; he who abides in Me and I in him, he bears much fruit, for apart from Me you can do nothing.

II. **The results of the believers' enjoyment and application of the divine dispensing of the Divine Trinity:**

   A. **Flowing the rivers of living water—John 7:38-39.**

   John 7:38-39
   He who believes in Me, as the Scripture said, out of his innermost being shall flow rivers of living water. (39) But this He said concerning the Spirit, whom those who believed in Him were about to receive; for the Spirit was not yet, because Jesus was not yet glorified.

   B. **Bearing the fruits of life—John 15:5, 16a.**

   John 15:5
   I am the vine, you are the branches; he who abides in Me and I in him, he bears much fruit, for apart from Me you can do nothing.

   John 15:16a
   You did not choose Me, but I chose you, and I appointed you that you should go forth and bear fruit...

   C. **Feeding the lambs in the flock—John 21:15; 10:16.**

   John 21:15
   Then when they had eaten breakfast, Jesus said to Simon Peter, Simon, son of John, do you

love Me more than these? He said to Him, Yes, Lord, You know that I love You. He said to him, Feed My lambs.

John 10:16
And I have other sheep which are not of this fold; I must bring them also, and they shall hear My voice, and there shall be one flock, one shepherd.

D. Becoming the bride of Christ, which is the Body of Christ as His increase—John 3:6b, 29-30.

John 3:6b
That which is born of the Spirit is spirit.

John 3:29-30
He who has the bride is the bridegroom; but the friend of the bridegroom, who stands and hears him, rejoices with joy because of the bridegroom's voice. This joy of mine therefore is made full. (30) He must increase, but I must decrease.

E. Being the organism of the processed Triune God—John 15:1, 5, 8.

John 15:1
I am the true vine, and My Father is the husbandman.

John 15:5
I am the vine, you are the branches; he who abides in Me and I in him, he bears much fruit, for apart from Me you can do nothing.

John 15:8
In this is My Father glorified, that you bear much fruit, and you shall become My disciples.

Prayer: Lord, we worship You from our depths. You are the Lord, the Source, and the Head. Thank You that You have gathered us into Your name once more tonight. We believe that You are here. We are here to seek You in Your Spirit. Lord, we believe that You will reveal Yourself to us in Your word. We are all here. May Your blood cleanse us in many ways, so that we may receive Your anointing and Your rich outpouring. Lord, calm our hearts, that we may be fully open to You, and may be fully delivered out of ourselves into Your Spirit. May Your Spirit grace every one of us here. Lord, operate in this meeting and in the depths of every one here, so that none would be left out and none would be left untouched, but that every one would have a word from You. Lord, may You be gracious to every one attending this meeting, no matter who he is. After this meeting is over, may we never forget it, but may we always remember our time of gathering here, and remember that it is here that we have met You and have been touched by You and have also touched You in our spirit. Lord, give us the living word and the rich supply. Transmit into us Your desire, Your love, Your thoughts, and even Your expression. Lord, may You be one spirit with us, and speak to us in our speaking. Lord, vindicate Your way, shame Your enemy, and bless every one who seeks after You. Amen!

THE PROCESSED TRIUNE GOD
FOR THE DIVINE DISPENSING

In the last message, we saw two main points. The first is the Divine Trinity, and the other is the divine dispensing. The Divine Trinity is our unique true God. He is the One we believe in, and the One we worship. With Him there is the distinction of the Father, the Son, and the Spirit. The Father is expressed in the Son, and the Son is realized as the Spirit. The Son is the manifestation of the Father, and the Spirit is the reality of the Son. These three are not three gods, but are one God. This unique God is the Father, the Son, and the Spirit for a definite purpose, which is to dispense Himself into His believers. He is one Triune God, yet He can be dispensed into millions of people. This is a mysterious thing. Although we have illustrated the dispensing of the Triune

God—the Father, the Son, and the Spirit—into us in the way of a watermelon being cut into pieces and then pressed into juice, the fact of the matter is not that simple. It is too profound. It is so profound that we cannot fathom it or understand it. Yet there is such a thing in the universe.

This Triune God had a pleasure and a desire in eternity past before the creation of the world. According to this pleasure and desire, the Divine Trinity had a conference of the Godhead and made the decision to create man in His image and according to His likeness, so that from one created man, He could propagate many men. Long before time began, and before the heavens and the earth were created, He predestinated us according to His foreknowledge and foresight and marked us out. In this way, we heard the gospel one day, and without knowing why we did so, we believed. Moreover, the more we go on, the more firmly we believe. Even we ourselves marvel and wonder how this happened. Actually, the whole matter is not up to us. We have been chosen by Him. Even if we do not want Him, He still wants us.

As far as we are concerned, salvation is merely a small experience. But as far as God is concerned, it is not a simple thing. First, He had to create all things. Then He had to create man. After the creation of man, because of man's failure, He had to wait four thousand years. In the end, He Himself became a man. In creating all things, He could call things not being into being. But in becoming flesh, He had to work according to the law of propagation which He created in man. One day, the Holy Spirit came to the virgin Mary, and a wonderful thing happened to her. A Holy One was conceived in her. The Holy One conceived in her was God, the eternal Word (Matt. 1:20). The God who was the Word entered the womb of the virgin Mary and remained there for nine months. At the completion of that time, He was born with a human nature. This was the Lord Jesus. What went in was God, and what came out at birth was God with humanity. This is what Isaiah 9:6 says, that a child is born to us, and a son is given to us. This child is the mighty God, and this Son is the eternal Father.

After the Lord Jesus was born, Herod tried to kill Him, and Joseph and Mary took him away to Egypt for refuge.

Later they returned to a small village in Galilee, Nazareth, where He spent thirty years in the house of a poor family. At the age of thirty, which according to Scripture is the age for a priest to assume his duties, He was baptized and was anointed by the Holy Spirit. Moreover, He was tested. From that time on, He began to speak for God and to work. Everywhere He went He spoke about God, expressed God, and revealed God to men. After three and a half years, He was betrayed, bound, and condemned, and He was crucified on the mount of Golgotha outside the city of Jerusalem. John told us that this crucified Jesus has three statuses. First, He is the Lamb of God, to be our Redeemer, taking away the sin of the world. Second, He is the brass serpent, hanged on the tree to remove the satanic nature within us. Third, He is the grain of wheat that fell into the ground and died, releasing the divine life and bearing the many grains.

Furthermore, His whole being—spirit, soul, and body—resurrected and was transfigured into the life-giving Spirit. This Spirit is a compound life-giving Spirit. In this Spirit there is divinity, humanity, the human living of Jesus, and His all-inclusive death with His resurrection power. This is the holy ointment described in Exodus 30. It is the mingling of one hin of olive oil with four kinds of spices. The Spirit as the holy ointment anointing us within enables us to partake of all the elements of the Triune God. In this way, through incarnation, human living, crucifixion, and resurrection to become the life-giving Spirit, the Triune God has achieved a great thing, which is to accomplish His divine dispensing. Today, our God is not simply the Word that was there in the beginning. He became flesh, worked for God on earth, went to the cross, accomplished the work of redemption, entered Hades, overcame death, and came out of death. In resurrection, He has become the life-giving Spirit. Now, He is so available to us. As long as we believe in Him and call on His name, He will dispense Himself into us. This is the gospel!

THE DIVINE DISPENSING BEING THE GOSPEL

Today, we should preach this gospel to others. We should not preach the shallow gospel that Christianity preaches.

That gospel tells people that they have sinned and must suffer the punishment of hell, but that God has had pity on them and has given His beloved Son to die for them to redeem them and to resurrect for them, and that as long as they repent and believe in Him, they will receive eternal life and will go to heaven. It tells them further that although the world is full of sufferings, they can trust in Him, learn to do good, and glorify God. Although this is the gospel, it is a low gospel. The high gospel that we preach says that the Word who was God from the beginning became flesh, passed through human living, was crucified, resurrected, and has become the life-giving Spirit to accomplish the great work of the divine dispensing.

Today, Jesus is not only our Redeemer and our Savior, He is also the dispensing God, dispensing Himself into all those who believe in Him. When He is dispensed into us, the believers, He becomes our grace and our reality, so that we have substance and are no longer empty. Our lives have a purpose and a goal. Since Christ has accomplished this divine dispensing and has become the life-giving Spirit and is now everywhere, He can enter into those that call on His name anytime and anywhere. At any time, when a person believes in Him and calls on His name, He will enter into this one and will become his life and everything to him.

I know definitely that I am saved. I also know definitely when I was saved. In April 1925, a young lady came from Shanghai to preach the gospel, and I went to listen out of curiosity. When I heard the word, I was caught by the Lord. There was no loud shouting, nor was there any jumping or skipping. I simply felt that I was captured by the Lord. I told the Lord that I did not want Satan to usurp me anymore. I did not want the world anymore. After the meeting, while I was on my way home, and before I reached home, I lifted up my head to heaven and said, "Lord, from today, even if the whole world is given to me, I will not take it anymore. I want to go and preach Jesus." After one or two years, I discovered that there was a change in me. The worldly entertainments that I formerly enjoyed were all shaken off from me. From that day on, I began to love the Lord, to pursue after Him, and to serve

Him. During my Christian life, very many things have confirmed to me that spiritual experiences are normal. The more normal the experience, the more proper it is. It is, in fact, miraculously normal. The reason for this is that the Triune God has been dispensed into me to be my life.

THE BELIEVERS' ENJOYMENT AND APPLICATION OF THE DIVINE DISPENSING OF THE DIVINE TRINITY

Regenerated to Receive God's Spirit of Life, Begetting into the Believers' Spirit That Which is the Life of Christ

After the Lord accomplished His divine dispensing, He sent men to preach the gospel. When we hear the gospel, our only choice is to believe. Once we believe and call on the name of the Lord, the following things happen. First, we are regenerated. When we receive the Lord, the dispensing of the Triune God begins to operate in us. The Spirit that was produced through the death and resurrection of the Lord Jesus enters into our spirit, and we receive God's Spirit of life, which begets into our spirit that which is the life of Christ (John 3:3-6). In other words, we receive the life of God in addition to our life in the flesh. From that point on, we are born of God and become God's children (John 1:12-13). God is our Father, and we are His household.

Breathing the Pneumatic Christ as Breath

Christ is not only our life to regenerate us. He is also the holy breath for our breathing. John 20:22 says that when the Lord Jesus came into the midst of the disciples, He said, "Receive the Holy Spirit." This means that every believer can breathe in the Lord through calling on His name. This breathing is the breathing in of the pneumatic Christ as air (John 20:22). Stanza 2 of *Hymns,* #73 says, "Just to breathe the Name of Jesus, is to drink of Life indeed."

Drinking the Pneumatic Christ as the Living Water

Third, to breathe in the name of the Lord Jesus is not only

to breathe in the Lord as air, but to drink of the pneumatic Christ as the living water (John 4:10, 14; 7:37-39). Hence, He is not only our life and our air, but also our living water.

Eating the Christ Who
Is in the Living Word of Life
as the Spiritual Food

In addition, we can eat the Christ who is in the living word of life as the spiritual food. The Lord said in John 6:63: "The words which I have spoken unto you are spirit and are life." It is this Spirit and this life that enables us to have the supply of the spiritual life. Second Timothy 3:16 also tells us that all Scripture is God-breathed. The word of God is the breathing out of God. What He breathes out, we breathe in. In this way, we will receive the supply of life.

Although the Bible contains many teachings and exhortations, when we receive them, we must first receive their supply, and then receive their teaching. Most people receive the teaching first. This is wrong. The Bible is the breath of God. It contains God's own element, and it is for our supply. In Romans 10:5-8 Paul quoted the word of the law in Deuteronomy 30:12-14. There he applied the word of the law to Christ, because although it was the word of the law, it came out of the mouth of God, and Christ is the One who came out of God. Hence, the written word of the Bible and the living word of Christ are both the word of God. When the Lord Jesus was tempted, three times He quoted the word of Deuteronomy to oppose Satan. He told the tempter that man shall not live on bread alone, but on every word that proceeds out of the mouth of God (Matt. 4:4). God's word can nourish man, because God's word is simply Christ.

Hence, when we read the Bible, we must first exercise our spirit to call on the Lord's name before we read. In this way, our spirit will receive the supply from Christ. Then when you try to understand the meaning of the Lord's word, you will receive more, because Christ will not only supply your spirit, but He will also open up your understanding and will enlighten your mind to comprehend the meaning of God's word. In the end, the supply you receive will not only be in your spirit, but will also be in your mind, emotion, and will. This is to eat Christ as the spiritual food.

Growing in the Bountiful Supply of Christ as the True Vine

Moreover, Christ is also the true vine. We are the branches of Him, the tree. When we abide in Him to enjoy all His riches, we will grow in His life. When we breathe Him in, eat Him, and drink of Him, His divine dispensing will enter into us to become our air, our living water, and our spiritual food. In this way, we will be able to abide in Him to enjoy the bountiful supply of Him as the vine.

From this, we can see that breathing, eating, and drinking Him is a kind of dispensing. Abiding in Him to absorb His riches is also a kind of dispensing. During the day, whenever it may be, as long as we turn to Him, His dispensing will go on within us.

For this reason, from now on, we have to change our concept. Not only can we pray-read two verses in the morning, but during the whole day we can always call on the Lord's name. As soon as we contact the Lord's word or call on His name, the supply comes. This is all the more necessary in the marriage life. No two persons living together can avoid problems. Therefore, I must tell you a spiritual principle: every time the other party makes you unhappy and causes you to lose your temper, you should tell yourself to call on the Lord Jesus first. This is the all-inclusive dose. The minute you call "O Lord Jesus," all the tempers are gone. Whenever we have any problem, the best way to deal with it is to call on the Lord.

If you ask me why I am so healthy, I can tell you that I always do one exercise, which is to walk around a little after I eat. Just a few steps render me great help. The same is true with our spiritual life. In the midst of our busy work, if we would stop for a while and would call on the Lord a little and think of Him a little, we would be strengthened. One hymn says that if we would say just a word to the Lord, everything would be well. Every time we encounter temptation, we need only to say a word to the Lord, and everything will be well. Whether it is the wife that is angry with the husband, or the husband that is wronged by the wife, there is no need to say even half a word to each other. As long as we say a word to the Lord, the temper will be gone. This is real and practical. We must not be affected by some teachings that say that one must fast or abstain from sleep before something will happen. All we need to do is to simply and consistently call on the Lord. Spontaneously, there will be a supply from the Lord's life. If we call on the Lord's name all the time, breathe Him in, drink Him, eat Him through the word of the Bible, and abide in Him to receive His supply, we will grow in the life of God.

THE RESULTS OF THE BELIEVERS' ENJOYMENT AND APPLICATION OF THE DIVINE DISPENSING OF THE DIVINE TRINITY

When we enjoy and apply the divine dispensing this way, five results will be manifested. First, out of us will flow rivers of living water (John 7:38-39). Second, we will bear fruits of life (John 15:5, 16a). Third, we will feed the lambs in the flock (John 21:15; 10:16). Fourth, we will become the bride of Christ, which is the Body of Christ as His increase (John 3:6b, 29-30). Fifth, we will become the organism of the processed Triune God to express the Triune God Himself (John 15:1, 5, 8). This is our Christian life. It is also the church life.

(A message given by Brother Witness Lee in Kota Kinabulu, Malaysia on October 25, 1990)

SECTION II

The Divine Dispensing of the Divine Trinity
in the Believers' Spirit, Soul, and Body
and Its Results and Goal

CHAPTER THREE

THE PROCESSED TRIUNE GOD CONSUMMATED TO BECOME THE LAW OF THE SPIRIT OF LIFE

OUTLINE AND SCRIPTURE READING

I. **The Spirit of life being the compound Spirit:**

   A. **Being a mingling of the divinity, humanity, human living, death, and resurrection of Christ with the Spirit of God to become the holy ointment—Exo. 30:23-25.**

   Exodus 30:23-25
   Take thou also unto thee principal spices, of pure myrrh five hundred shekels, and of sweet cinnamon half so much, even two hundred and fifty shekels, and of sweet calamus two hundred and fifty shekels, (24) and of cassia, five hundred shekels, after the shekel of the sanctuary, and of oil olive a hin: (25) and thou shalt make it an oil of holy ointment, an ointment compound after the art of the apothecary: it shall be a holy anointing oil.

   B. **The supplying element of this compound Spirit being bountiful and excellent—Phil. 1:19b.**

   Philippians 1:19b
   ...the bountiful supply of the Spirit of Jesus Christ.

II. **The law of this Spirit of life being the consummated Triune God—Rev. 22:17a:**

Revelation 22:17a
And the Spirit and the bride say, Come!

A. **Becoming the law of life with its natural life-capacities and its spontaneous life-power—Rom. 8:2a.**

Romans 8:2a
For the law of the Spirit of life in Christ Jesus...

B. **Freeing the believers from the law of sin and of death, solving for them the problem of sin and of death—Rom. 8:2b.**

Romans 8:2b
...has freed me from the law of sin and of death.

THE ETERNAL ECONOMY OF THE TRIUNE GOD

In Paul's Epistles, and especially in the book of Romans, 1 and 2 Corinthians, and Ephesians, we see that before the ages, that is, in eternity past, God had a desire and a pleasure. His desire and pleasure became His motive, which gave Him a purpose, a plan, and an arrangement in eternity. Paul called this purpose, plan, and arrangement God's economy. God's economy is to gain a group of people and to work Himself into them so that He can be their life and everything to them and can mingle Himself as one with them in their living. In this way, He lives within them, and they live out His glory. By this, He is expressed.

This expression is, on the one hand, individual and, on the other hand, corporate. Individually speaking, we the believers have God's life to live God's glorious living, that is, a living that lives out God Himself. Corporately speaking, when the saints come together, they live a living that glorifies God, which is the church life. This corporate expression is what God is really after.

In order to accomplish this economy, God must be triune. He is not merely God, but He is the Triune God—the Father, the Son, and the Spirit. We call this the Divine Trinity. The Father is the source; the Son is the expression, manifested among us; and the Spirit is the reaching to us and the entrance into us of the Triune God. The Father is in the Son, the Son becomes the Spirit, and the Spirit enters into us to be the reality of the Triune God. When the Spirit comes, the Son comes, and the Father also comes. Hence, the Spirit is the totality of the Divine Trinity and is also the ultimate consummation of the Divine Trinity. The Father is expressed in the Son. The Son is realized as the Spirit. The Spirit is the reality of the Triune God coming to us and entering into us to be our life. He is mingled with us and shares with us the same living.

THE DIVINE DISPENSING OF THE DIVINE TRINITY

In the New Testament, the first book that speaks expressly about this subject is the Gospel of John. At the very beginning, it tells us that in the beginning was the Word, and the Word was with God, and the Word was God (John 1:1). One day, this Word became flesh, bringing with Him grace and reality in fullness (John 1:14). In addition, this Word is the Lamb of God that takes away the sin of the world (John 1:29). He is also the brass serpent that was lifted up and that destroyed Satan (John 3:14). He is even the grain of wheat that fell into the ground and died. Through His death and resurrection, the divine life was released from within Him, and it entered into us, the believers, producing the many grains (John 12:24) that are ground into flour and made into a loaf. This loaf is the Body of Christ.

Furthermore, when He entered into resurrection, He changed His form from that of the flesh to that of the Spirit. First Corinthians 15:45 says that this Christ has become the life-giving Spirit. This Spirit is also the Spirit of life described in Romans 8:2. This means that He is the Spirit and He is life as well. On the night of the resurrection, the Lord Jesus came into the midst of the disciples and appeared to them. He greeted them and breathed into them a holy breath, that they would receive the Holy Spirit (John 20:19-22). The Word who was God in the beginning has become flesh, passed through death, entered into resurrection, and become ultimately this holy breath, which is the Holy Spirit. Today, He is such a One in the universe. He is the holy breath, the Holy Spirit, the God who has entered into us to be our life. If we receive Him, we will be regenerated; that is, we will receive the life of God in addition to having our life in the flesh. He is our holy breath; we can breathe Him in. He is also the living water; we can drink Him in. He is the spiritual food in God's word; we can eat Him. Moreover, we can abide in Him and can allow Him to abide in us. In this way, we will grow, we can bear the fruit of life, and out from us there will flow rivers of living water.

There is a hymn that says, "The Spirit begets the spirit, the spirit worships the Spirit, so that the Spirit fills me up. The Spirit becomes the word, bringing with Him the abundant life, flowing out of us as the rivers of living water." This is the Gospel of John. God's economy is very deep and profound;

yet John used very simple words to explain these profound things. However, he did not touch the limit or the peak. Hence, in addition to him, there is Paul. Paul's fourteen Epistles, found after the Gospel of John, speak of God's economy. He told us in a rich and profound way how the Divine Trinity, the Father, the Son, and the Spirit, passed through the many processes to come to us, to be with us, and even to enter into us to be our life. He lives in us so that we can become the means for Him to be lived out. When we come together, we are the church, living a life that glorifies God and expresses God.

THE FOUR LAWS

We can say that the main thing Paul's Epistles cover is the mystery of the divine dispensing of the Divine Trinity. At the beginning of Romans, Paul speaks in a simple way about God's creation of the heavens and the earth. After His creation of man, man became fallen before God and has a history of sin. God then gave the law to expose man's sinful condition before Him. Under God's condemnation, man appears corrupted and poor. Thank God, Christ came and accomplished redemption for us. He was resurrected in the Father's glory, and He delivered us out of sin and death so that we can live in the newness of God's life. This is what Romans 1 to 6 covers. From chapter seven on, Paul begins to speak in depth about the mystery.

The Law of Good in the Mind

He told us that with the Triune God—the Father, the Son, and the Spirit—the Father is in the Son, the Son has become the Spirit, who is the Spirit of life, and this Spirit of life has a law. We know that when we throw objects into the air, they will come back down by themselves. This is because of gravitational force, which is a law. Based on his spiritual experience, Paul discovered that there is a law in the universe, which is the law of the Spirit of life. Romans 7 and 8 present a clear explanation of this law. In these two chapters, four laws are mentioned. The first is the law of good in man's mind. When God created man, He created him according to His own image, that is, according to what He is: love, light, holiness, and righteousness. Hence, the man He created was the same as He is, having love, light, holiness, and righteousness within. The only difference is that His love, light, holiness, and righteousness are divine, whereas our love, light, holiness, and righteousness are human. Man was created by God in this way, with the human life and the law of this human life.

Every living creature has its law of life. For example, when the peach tree bears fruit, surely they are peaches. This is the law of the peach tree. The peach tree brings forth peaches, and the pear tree brings forth pears. The cat begets cats, and the dog begets dogs. Every life has its own law. The human life is created by God; it is the highest life among all creatures. Of course this life also has its law. Although our ancestor sinned and has caused man to fall into sin, deep within us there is still love, light, holiness, and righteousness. We do not want to be wrong, and we do not want to be in darkness. We want to do good, and we desire to act in light. This shows us, indeed, that man wants to do good. On the one hand, we are corrupt. On the other hand, we still want to do good. Deep within every one of us, there is a heart for doing good. This is what Paul meant by the law of good in our mind.

The Law of Sin in Man's Flesh

Second, there is the law of sin in man's flesh. After man fell by eating of the tree of the knowledge of good and evil, there was another law in his flesh. This law is also a life, but it is neither God's life nor man's life. Rather, it is the evil life of Satan. When this life enters into man, he has Satan's nature, and he inherits another law, which is the law of evil and sin. Paul said in Romans 7:19-21, "For the good which I will, I do not; but the evil I do not will, this I practice. But if what I do not will, this I do, it is no longer I that do it but sin that dwells in me. I find then the law that, at my willing to do the good, the evil is present with me". Moreover, this law was constantly warring with the law of good in Paul's mind, making him a captive and causing him to do evil (Rom. 7:23).

The Law of God

As far as God's creation is concerned, we are good. But as

far as man's fall is concerned, we are evil. Among the ancient Chinese philosophers, some said that man's nature is good, and others said that man's nature is evil. Actually, both are right. In a fallen man, there are these two opposing laws, one that compels him to do good, and the other that compels him to do evil. However, man does not necessarily know himself in this way. For this reason, God gave the law, which is the Ten Commandments, which exposes man's true condition. The law of these Ten Commandments is the third kind of law. The sum total of this law is that God is a God of love, light, holiness, and righteousness. He forbids man to worship idols, and He tells man to honor his parents, not to kill, steal, commit fornication, or be covetous. In other words, He wants man to have love, light, holiness, and righteousness. God uses this law to expose man from without. After man is exposed, he becomes willing to walk by the law of God. However, when he sets out to keep the law, he discovers that it is not up to himself. He fails, and he is made a captive of Satan to do that which he does not will. He wills to love, but instead he hates. He wills to be in the light, but instead he is in darkness. He wills to be holy, but instead he is defiled by worldliness. He wills to be righteous, but instead he becomes unjust and unrighteous. Therefore, Paul drew a conclusion: "For to will is present with me, but to do the good is not" (Rom. 7:18b). Again he said, "Wretched man that I am! Who will deliver me from the body of this death?" (Rom. 7:24).

The Law of the Spirit of Life

Paul finally knew himself. But he did not remain there. He discovered that in him there is still a fourth law. The first is the law of good in man's mind. The second is the law of evil in man's flesh. The third is the law of God given by God outside of man. The fourth is found only in those who have believed in the Lord Jesus Christ. It is the law of the Spirit of life. Because we are created beings, we have the human law of good. Because we have become fallen, we have the evil law of Satan. Because we are before God, we also have God's law. Prior to our believing in the Lord, there were these three laws: one in the mind, that desires to do good; one in the flesh, that compels us to do evil; and one outside of us, that puts a demand on us. God requires that we have love, light, holiness, and righteousness, but we cannot have them. For this reason, we repent, confess our sins, and believe in the Lord Jesus. Once we believe in Him, God comes into us to be our life. With this life there is a law. It is not the law of good, nor the law of evil. Neither is it the law of God outside of man. Rather, it is the law of the Spirit of life. This law of the Spirit of life is the Triune God Himself. The living Person of the Triune God is our life within us. This life has a law, which is called the law of the Spirit of life. Life, Spirit, and the law—these three are just one thing. This law is the Spirit, and this Spirit is life.

THE SPIRIT OF LIFE BEING THE COMPOUND SPIRIT

Exodus 30:23-25 speaks of the compound holy ointment. The compound holy ointment is composed of one hin of olive oil with four spices. The one hin of oil signifies the unique God. Olive oil signifies the Spirit of God flowing out through the pressing of the death of Christ. It is the base of the ointment, and it is the basic ingredient in which the spices are mingled. The four spices signify humanity in God's creation with the precious death of Christ, the sweetness and effectiveness of His death, the resurrection of Christ, and the power and fragrance of resurrection, respectively. Hence, this compound ointment signifies the Spirit produced out of the Lord's death and resurrection. In this Spirit, there is divinity, humanity, the Lord's death, resurrection, and His redemption. The supplying element of this compound Spirit is both bountiful and excellent (Phil. 1:19b).

THE LAW OF THE SPIRIT OF LIFE BEING
THE ULTIMATE CONSUMMATION OF THE TRIUNE GOD

Today, we the sinners need only to repent, believe in the Lord Jesus, and call on His name. The all-inclusive, compound, life-giving Spirit will enter into us to be our life, and there will be a wonderful change. By this, we will be regenerated. We will no longer be ourselves, but we will have the Lord Jesus within us. Before we are saved, we are just our own selves, Malaysian or Chinese. But after we are saved, though we may still look like the same persons, actually, within us, another One is added, who is the Lord Jesus. As far as our natural constitution goes, we are all different from one another. There are the Malaysians, the Chinese, and the Americans. But after we have believed in the Lord and been saved, as far as the inner man goes, we are all the same; we are all people with God within us. God is the Spirit, life, and also the law within us. Now, within every Christian there is a law, which is the law of the all-inclusive and life-giving Spirit produced through the Triune God passing through incarnation, human living, crucifixion, death, and resurrection. This law of the Spirit of life is the ultimate consummation of the Triune God (Rev. 22:17a).

We know that an airplane can fly smoothly because it has power that overcomes the force of gravity. If I am on an airplane and am seated properly with the safety belt fastened in place, would I not be a fool if I still hold onto the seat tightly and fear that I will fall down? In the same way, after we have believed in the Lord Jesus, it is wrong for us to try to do anything by our own effort. To believe in the Lord Jesus can be compared to riding on an airplane. All we have to do is to sit in our seats at ease. We do not need to try to fly, nor do we need to try to hold onto anything, because we are not the ones that are flying, but it is the airplane that is flying. The same is true with spiritual matters. Once we are on the airplane, who is Christ, we should not try to fly anymore. Instead, we should let Christ fly us away. We should abandon all the struggling and striving and allow Christ to be the Lord and everything to us.

Having the Natural Life-capacity with the Spontaneous Life-power

In our daily life, we often pray to the Lord for victory and revival. This is like trying to fly by ourselves. We should pray to the Lord: "Lord, You are my revival. You are my victory. I cannot revive myself, nor can I be victorious." Do not pray for victory anymore. Instead, you should be like Paul, praising and thanking the Lord. He said in 2 Corinthians 2:14, "But thanks be to God, who always leads us in triumph in the Christ." We must always remember that we have boarded Christ, our "airplane." This airplane has its law, and once the law begins to operate, the airplane flies into the air. I am afraid that, doctrinally speaking, we are allowing Christ to fly for us. But actually, we are still trying to fly by ourselves. This is the reason we always fail.

The law of the Spirit of life in Romans 8 has a capacity which operates in us daily to revive us and to allow us to overcome. I have no intention to exhort you to be revived every morning or to overcome every day by yourselves. But I do want to remind you of the two simple words in the New Testament: "in Christ." Today, Christ Himself is the law of the Spirit of life within us. We do not need to be revived and to overcome by ourselves, and we do not need to strive by ourselves to do good. All we need to say is, "Lord, I love You." The first thing we should say every morning is, "Lord, I love You. I offer myself to You." This matches the teaching of Romans. Romans 6:13 tells us to present ourselves to God, and to present our members as weapons of righteousness to God. If you truly present yourselves to God and cooperate with Him, in your daily life you will realize that you are in Christ, and that there is a law operating within you. This law has a natural life-capacity and a spontaneous life-power (Rom. 8:2).

It is very easy for us to be weak and sometimes to be confused. For this reason, we have to call on the Lord Jesus continually. Whenever you are weak or feel lacking, you should call, "O Lord Jesus." As long as you would call softly from your heart and fellowship with Him, you will come alive within. This is our Christian life. In this message, I wish to give you an impression, which is that every saved person should be one who presents himself to the Lord. Hence, every morning when we wake up, we have to renew an exercise of saying, "Lord, I love You. I want to present myself to You." You should do this in the morning and should continue this during the day. When you encounter difficulties or trials, you should especially learn to call from the depths of your being, "O Lord Jesus!" If you contact the Lord this way, you will come alive within and will be strengthened.

RELEASING THE BELIEVERS
FROM THE LAW OF SIN AND OF DEATH,
AND SOLVING FOR THEM THE PROBLEM
OF SIN AND DEATH

In our daily lives, it is difficult for us not to come into conflict with others or not to encounter unhappy incidences. How can we overcome in these circumstances? The way is not to make resolutions or to struggle, but to call on the Lord. Every morning when we wake up, we should call, "Lord, I love You. I give myself to You." After this, we should open the Bible to pray-read two verses. In this way, even if there are things in our daily life that may stir up our temper, we will not be stirred up, and even if there are things that may cause anxiety, we will not be anxious. This is the Christian life. Do not think that this is too simple, and do not think that this is superstitious. Even more, do not think that this is a mental illusion. In the universe there is only one name. The more you call on it, the sweeter you will feel, and the more you will overcome. This is our Lord Jesus. If we call on Him a little, we will be overcomers. There is no need for us to beg or to ask the Lord for help. All we have to do is to present ourselves to the Lord and to cooperate with Him, allowing the law of the Spirit of life to have a chance to operate within us.

We were born in sin, and we grew up in death. The law of sin and of death is within us. But we have been delivered from it already. Thank the Lord, "For the law of the Spirit of life in Christ Jesus has freed me from the law of sin and of death" (Rom. 8:2). We have been delivered from the sphere of Adam and have been transferred into the realm of Christ. In Christ there is not the law of sin and of death, but the law of the Spirit of life. Now, everything has become a matter of a law. We do not need to struggle or to strive. We only need to remain in Christ, to present ourselves to Him, to give Him the freedom, and to enjoy Him. In this way, He will gain our cooperation and will operate in us spontaneously and gently. By this, we will have peace, joy, and victory.

(A message given by Brother Witness Lee in Sibu, Malaysia on October 26, 1990)

A SUPPLEMENTARY WORD

(1)

THE ACCOMPLISHMENT
OF THE DIVINE DISPENSING

The Divine Trinity has passed through many processes for His divine dispensing. First, He came from heaven on high to the earth and was conceived in the womb of a virgin. There He remained for nine months according to the law of the human life, and He was born as a God-man. Because of King Herod's jealousy, He escaped to Egypt and later returned to settle in Galilee, living in the little town of Nazareth. In a hidden way, He lived there for thirty years. No one heard of Him or knew Him. When He was thirty years old, He came out to fulfill His ministry, which was to seek and to save the lost sinners and to dispense God into them.

One day, He was returning from Jerusalem to Galilee. According to His foreknowledge and predestination, He went to save a lost sinner, an immoral Samaritan woman. For this, He purposely went through Samaria and waited for the woman by the well at Sychar. He knew that the woman would go to draw water at that hour. When the Lord Jesus met her, He asked her for water in order to point out her real need. He spoke to her about her husband. By this He touched her conscience so that she would repent for her sins. In addition, the Lord showed her that true worship is to drink of God as the living water and to contact in spirit God who is the Spirit. The Chinese way of worship is to kneel down three times with the head touching the ground nine times. The Arab way of worship is to prostrate the whole body. But our God does not want us to worship in either of these ways. He wants us to worship in spirit and in reality, which is to drink of Him as the thirst-quenching living water. If we drink of the water from the well of Jacob, we will be thirsty again. Our thirst can never be satisfied by the earthly water. Only God's gift of Jesus as our living water can give us satisfaction in life.

Hence, every Lord's Day our breaking of bread for the remembrance of the Lord is not a form of worship, but an eating, drinking, and enjoyment of God. The symbols on the table—the bread and the cup—signify the Lord's body that was broken for us and the new covenant that was enacted by the Lord's blood. They are there for us to eat, drink, and enjoy. We do this in remembrance of the Lord (Matt. 26:26-28; Luke 22:19). Hence, the Lord does want us to remember Him. But He does not want us to kneel down and to think about Him in silence. Rather, He wants us to open ourselves up and to contact Him with our spirit, eating and drinking Him in spirit. This is the true remembrance of Him.

In the past messages we have seen that in eternity past, God had an economy. In order to accomplish this economy, He passed through many processes to dispense Himself to us. From His incarnation to His becoming the life-giving Spirit, every step was for the accomplishment of His dispensing. Take the crucifixion for an example. Man hanged Him on the cross for six hours. In the first three hours, He was persecuted for the carrying out of God's will. In the last three hours, He was judged by God for the accomplishment of redemption on our behalf. This death was indeed a process which accomplished many works. After this, He entered into death and Hades. Three days later, He resurrected. This was another process. As soon as He entered resurrection, He was transfigured to become the life-giving Spirit. By that time, all the processes that He had to go through were completed.

The whole Gospel of John shows us this matter clearly. At the start of the book, it says that in the beginning was the Word, and the Word was God. The Word became flesh. Later it shows us how the incarnated God-man Jesus lived on the earth for thirty-three and a half years. In the end, He was crucified and entered Hades; then He came out again to enter into resurrection. In resurrection He became the life-giving

Spirit, who is the holy breath breathed into the disciples. In this way, they all received the Holy Spirit.

THE DISPENSING OF THE DIVINE TRINITY TO THE BELIEVERS

Today, the One that we believe in and worship is such a One. He has become the Spirit, the ultimate consummation of the Triune God, for the purpose that we would partake of His divine dispensing. This is the mysterious economy of God, which is to dispense and to distribute to God's children all the rich elements of God. Now this God has been processed and has become a holy breath, everywhere filling the earth. Even while you are preaching the gospel to others, He is in your mouth and in your heart. He will come out of your heart and will enter the mouth of those who listen (Romans 10:8-9). He is the Holy Spirit, the Triune God, Jesus Christ, becoming life and everything to those who believe and receive Him. He is so wonderful.

This wonderful One is in us mainly to be our life, operating and working quietly and gently in us. This can be compared to our physical life. Every day, twenty-four hours a day, it operates quietly and gently in us. While we are sitting here, an operation is working within, which is our digestion. However, we do not feel it. Whenever we feel it, that proves that there is something wrong with us. Not only is there the digestion, but there is the assimilation as well, which makes the digested food elements part of our blood and constitutes these elements as the cells and tissues of our body. When God's Spirit works in us, He operates in a similar way.

He is coming to us not only to be our life, but to be our everything, that is, to be our person. He wants to abide in us, to make home and to settle down in our whole being so that He can become our all. He is waiting all the time within us for us to turn to Him and to receive His supply. Some always speak of the Lord's dealing with them and His rebuking of them. But in my experience of sixty or more years of following the Lord, it seems that the Lord never has rebuked me severely. I have indeed offended Him many times. But He is always willing to supply me and to dispense Himself into me.

Today, the Lord is definitely living in me. He is our life, to be our everything. He is our person, our Head, our Husband, and our Savior. He wants to make His home in us and to make our whole person His place of rest.

I have to ask the young ones sitting here among us: is the Lord a guest or the host in you today? Are you His home? Our natural concept is to improve or adjust the negative or bad things. After we believed in the Lord, we thought that the Lord was here to improve us and to make us a noble person. Actually, this is not the case. Before being saved, we sinned and made mistakes easily. After someone preached the gospel to us, we realized that we were sinners and that we needed a Savior. As a result, we accepted the Lord Jesus. He has died on the cross for us and borne our sins, accomplishing redemption, and He has become our Redeemer. He is even our Savior day by day. Although we are saved, we still have many weaknesses, lusts, and passions. At the same time, we are continually faced with many trials and sufferings. For this reason, we need His daily salvation so that we can be a person with God and can live a life that is above that of ordinary men.

THE DIVINE DISPENSING
"DEIFYING" THE BELIEVERS

Over twenty years ago, when I first came to the United States, I told the brothers that even if our ancestor Adam had not fallen and we had not sinned, we would still need to be regenerated. The reason for this is that God wanted to have many sons who would have His life and who would be His expression. Although He created man perfect and flawless, He Himself had not come into man and had not been joined to man. If man were merely perfect but did not have God within, this would still be short of what God wants. When God created man, He created him as a vessel. However, he was but an empty vessel. God's purpose is to fill up this vessel with Himself. However, before God filled man up, man became defiled and corrupted. Hence, God came to redeem man and cleanse him. But this is only the means; it is not God's goal. God's ultimate desire is to enter into the created man to be his life so that he would gain Him and be joined and mingled with Him to live God's living. For this purpose, He first came to be a man, to "man-ize" Himself. Then He enables us to partake of His life, thus to "God-ize" us. In this way, He and we become one and share one living.

This concept is not found in Christianity. Although the Bible does contain this truth, those in Christianity have not been able to see it. This can be compared to reading a book. If there are words that we do not understand, no matter how many times we read through it, we will not be able to understand its true meaning, and we will not be very concerned about its significance. The ultimate purpose of God is to work Himself into us that He may be our life and everything to us so that one day we can become Him. But this does not mean that we can become part of the Godhead and be the same as the unique God. We have to know that although we are born of God and have God's life to become God's children, His house, and His household, we do not have a share in His sovereignty or His Person and cannot be worshiped as God.

In church history, beginning from the second century, some church fathers who were expounding the Bible used the term deification, which means to make man God. Later they were opposed by others and were considered as heretics. But John 1:12-13 does say, "But as many as received Him, to them He gave authority to become children of God, to those who believe in His name: who were born not of blood, nor of the will of the flesh, nor of the will of man, but of God." We the believers are begotten of God. What is begotten of man is man, and what is begotten of God must be God. We are born of God; hence, in this sense, we are God. Nevertheless, we must know that we do not share God's Person and cannot be worshiped by others. Only God Himself has the Person of God and can be worshiped by man.

THE DIVINE DISPENSING
MAKING THE BELIEVERS GOD-MEN

The traditional concept in Christianity is that God wants us, the saved ones, to be good, to be spiritual, and to be holy, but there is no concept that God wants us to be God-men.

When God became flesh and came to earth, He was both God and man, a wonderful God-man, having both divinity and humanity. As for us, we are not only created by Him, but we have Him begotten into us, so that every one of us has God's life and nature, and we are now God's children (2 Pet. 1:4). Therefore, as those begotten of God, we are all God-men.

My burden is to show you clearly that God's economy and plan is to make Himself man and to make us, His created beings, "God," so that He is "man-ized" and we are "God-ized." In the end, He and we, we and He, all become God-men. Hence, it is not enough for us to be good men, spiritual men, or holy men. These are not what God is after. What God wants today is God-men. God does not expect us to improve ourselves, because God is not after our being good men. He wants us to be God-men. He is our life and everything to us for the purpose that we would express Him and live Him out.

When God created us, He created us according to His image and after His likeness. We are like a picture, which has His image, but is without His life. After we are regenerated, this picture becomes the "real" person, having His life and nature, and being the same as He is. He is God "man-ized," and we are man "God-ized." In the end, the two become one, both being God-men. This is the divine revelation of the Bible.

For this reason, we have to exercise ourselves to be God-men. To improve oneself is worth little. God is not here to improve man, but to beget man. God begot us so that we can receive His life and nature and can grow in His life. When God grows within us, we grow (Col. 2:19). In order for God to increase within us, we have to exercise our spirit, because every proper thing that goes on between God and man depends on the spirit. The more we exercise our spirit, the more God operates and increases within us. As a result, we grow up to become genuine God-men. This is what God is after.

(A message given by Brother Witness Lee in Sibu, Malaysia on October 27, 1990)

CHAPTER FOUR

THE OPERATION AND THE DISPENSING OF THE LAW OF THE SPIRIT OF LIFE IN THE THREE PARTS OF THE BELIEVERS

OUTLINE AND SCRIPTURE READING

I. **Beginning from the believers' spirit:**

A. **By God's Spirit dwelling in the believers—Rom. 8:9a.**

   Romans 8:9a
   But you are not in the flesh, but in the spirit, if indeed the Spirit of God dwells in you.

B. **The Spirit of Christ, that is, the pneumatic Christ, making home in the believers' spirit—Rom. 8:9b-10a.**

   Romans 8:9b-10a
   But if anyone has not the Spirit of Christ, he is not of Him. (10a) And if Christ is in you...

C. **That the believers, though dead in their bodies because of sin, may have their spirits become life because of righteousness—Rom. 8:10b.**

   Romans 8:10b
   ...though the body is dead because of sin, yet the spirit is life because of righteousness.

II. **Continuing in the believers' soul:**

A. **By the believers setting the mind of their soul on the spirit—Rom. 8:6b.**

   Romans 8:6b
   ...but the mind set on the spirit is life and peace.

B. **That the divine dispensing that dwells in the believers' spirit may spread into the believers' soul, that their mind may be transformed and their soul renewed—Rom. 12:2b.**

Romans 12:2b
...be transformed by the renewing of the mind, that you may prove by testing what the will of God is, that which is good and well-pleasing and perfect.

III. **Consummated in the believers' body:**

A. **By the Spirit of the One who raised Christ from the dead dwelling in the believers' spirit and soul—Rom. 8:11a.**

Romans 8:11a
But if the Spirit of Him who raised Jesus from among the dead dwells in you...

B. **That He who raised Christ from the dead may spread His divine dispensing into the believers' body through His indwelling Spirit—Rom. 8:11b.**

Romans 8:11b
...He who raised Christ Jesus from among the dead will also give life to your mortal bodies through His Spirit who indwells you.

C. **That the believers' mortal body may also receive the supply and saturation of the divine life—Rom. 8:11b.**

Romans 8:11b
...He who raised Christ Jesus from among the dead will also give life to your mortal bodies through His Spirit who indwells you.

Prayer: Lord, we praise and thank You that You are here with us. We believe that You will speak to us in Your Spirit. Lord, may You speak more. Speak within us, and speak through our speaking. May there be word upon word and Spirit upon Spirit so that every one of us would meet You and be touched by You. May You gain the glory. May Satan be shamed, and may the saints be blessed. Amen!

GOD BEING TRIUNE

These messages are on Romans 8. Romans 8 can be considered as the most profound chapter in the Bible. It is profound in two aspects: first, our God is the Triune God, the Father, the Son, and the Spirit; second, this Triune God is working Himself into our tripartite being. According to the revelation of the Bible, God is triune. He is the Father, the Son, and the Spirit. This means that the One whom we serve, worship, believe in, receive, and live by is the Triune God. This Triune God has a very profound distinction: He is the unique God, yet He is of three persons. That is why He is called the Triune God.

The word *triune* does not seem to be an accurate mathematical number. This word comes from Latin and is formed from two words: *tri*, which means *three*, and *une*, which means *one*. Therefore, the word triune means three-one.

According to the record of the Bible, before the Lord Jesus became flesh, and even before His resurrection, He had never revealed to man the Divine Trinity. It was not until He passed through incarnation, human living, crucifixion, death, and resurrection that He revealed this matter to man. When He entered into resurrection, He immediately became the life-giving Spirit. This is a tremendous thing. Let me say this again: Christ is the embodiment of the Triune God who has passed through incarnation, human living, crucifixion, and resurrection. In resurrection He became the life-giving Spirit. This Spirit is the Spirit of life described in Romans 8. Before His ascension, He appeared to His disciples and charged them: "And Jesus came and spoke to them, saying, All authority has been given to Me in heaven and on earth. Go therefore and disciple all the nations, baptizing them into the name of the Father and of the Son and of the Holy Spirit" (Matt. 28:18-19). The name in which people are to be baptized is the name of the Father and of the Son and of the Holy Spirit. The Father, the Son, and the Spirit are three, yet the name is one. There are three persons with only one name. This name is the aggregate title of the Divine Being. It represents the Triune God Himself.

THE TRIUNE GOD— THE FATHER, THE SON, AND THE SPIRIT

John 1:1 says, "In the beginning was the Word, and the Word was with God, and the Word was God." From this, we can see that the Word can never be separated from God. The two are one. The Word is the definition, explanation, and expression of God. This Word not only speaks forth God, but speaks God into man, because this Word is the defined, explained, and expressed God. One day this Word became flesh (John 1:14). The One who became flesh was the Word, who was God, the complete Triune God. For the Word to become flesh is for the Triune God to become a man of flesh. In this way, He became a sinless God-man, being the complete God as well as the perfect man, having divinity as well as humanity. This is Jesus. This is also the Triune God.

This God-man Jesus remained on earth with the disciples for three and a half years. One day, His disciple Philip said to Him, "Lord, show us the Father and it suffices us" (John 14:8). After the Lord Jesus heard this, He answered, "Am I so long a time with you, and you have not known Me, Philip? He who has seen Me has seen the Father....The words which I speak to you, I do not speak from Myself; but the Father who abides in Me, He does His works" (John 14:9-10). The Lord was rebuking Philip and seemed to be saying, "Why do you ask Me? Don't you know that I am just the Father?" This shows us that the Second of the Triune God, the Son, is the First of the Triune God, the Father. The Son is the Father.

After this, the Lord Jesus said, "And I will ask the Father, and He will give you another Comforter, that He may be with you forever; even the Spirit of reality...He abides with you and shall be in you. I will not leave you orphans; I am coming to you" (John 14:16-18). This Spirit of reality is just the Lord Himself. This shows that the Christ in the flesh has passed through death and resurrection to become the Spirit of life. This Spirit of life is the pneumatic Christ. This Spirit is the reality of Christ (1 John 5:6, 20), making Christ real in the believers. Hence, the Third of the Triune God, the Spirit, is also the reality of the Second, the Son. Furthermore, the Lord Jesus told the disciples, "In that day you shall know that I am in My Father, and you in Me, and I in you" (John 14:20). *That day* refers to the day of the Lord's resurrection. On the day of His resurrection, the Third of the Triune God, the Spirit, who is the other Comforter, came into the disciples with all the reality of the Triune God to abide in them. At that time, the disciples knew that the Son was in the Father, the disciples were in the Son, and the Son was in the disciples. Because the Son is in the Father, when the Son comes into us, the Father also comes into us. The Triune God—the Father, the Son, and the Spirit—are joined as one with us, the believers.

The Triune God and the Tripartite Man

John revealed to us in his Gospel that the God whom we worship, serve, believe in, and live by is the Triune God—the Father, the Son, and the Spirit. Paul also revealed to us in his epistles that we who are created by God are tripartite men, composed of spirit, soul, and body. The Triune God—the Father, the Son, and the Spirit—is mysterious and is not simple at all. The three parts of our being—the spirit, the soul, and the body—also are mysterious and are not simple. When we go to school to receive an education, we are satisfying the need of the soul, so that we can have a strong soul. In school we also do physical exercises. This is to meet the need of the body, so that we can have a strong body. But though we study and engage in physical activities, we often feel empty. This is because our spirit is not satisfied. Our spirit needs to be filled by God. We need God. Only God can "light up" our spirit. If we are right in all three parts of our being, we will be persons who are healthy in our body, strong in our soul, and bright in our spirit.

In Romans 8:9-10 Paul said, "But you are not in the flesh, but in the spirit, if indeed the Spirit of God dwells in you. But if anyone has not the Spirit of Christ, he is not of Him. And if Christ is in you, though the body is dead because of sin, yet the spirit is life because of righteousness." Here we can see that the Spirit of God is just the Spirit of Christ. The two are one Spirit, and Christ is these two Spirits. Hence, the Spirit of God, the Spirit of Christ, and Christ Himself—the three—are one. After this, Paul said, "But if the Spirit of Him who raised Jesus from among the dead dwells in you, He who raised Christ Jesus from among the dead will also give life to your mortal bodies through His Spirit who indwells you" (Rom. 8:11). This means that if we allow the Spirit of the Triune God to dwell in us, in our experience we will not be in the flesh but in the spirit. If that is the case, He as the Spirit will spread from our spirit to our soul, represented by the mind, and will finally give life even to our mortal body.

THE DISPENSING OF THE TRIUNE GOD
INTO THE TRIPARTITE MAN

How does the Triune God—the Father, the Son, and the Spirit—work Himself into the tripartite man of spirit, soul, and body? First, Christ enters into our spirit and makes our spirit alive. At this time our soul is still dead because of sin. Next, if we set our mind on the spirit continually, the Spirit will enter into our mind, so that our mind will be filled with the Spirit and will become the divine life. In this way, not only our spirit will have life; our mind also will have life. Finally, He who raised Christ from among the dead will give life to our mortal body through the Spirit of resurrection, who dwells in us, so that we will have life also in our body. First, there is life in the spirit. Then there is life in our soul. Finally, there is life for our body. This is how the Triune God dispenses Himself into the tripartite man. This is also the greatest and the most profound mystery in the universe.

We are all tripartite persons with a spirit, a soul, and a body. We not only need to be strong in our soul and body; we need to be bright in our spirit as well. Only in this way can we be directed and led by the Spirit of God, and only then will we be a proper person who is useful to our family, relatives, friends, society, and country. Such a person has gained God and is gained by God. Before we believed in the Lord, our body might not have been very proper. Our soul was not good, and our spirit was darkened and dead. However, thank the Lord, we have believed in Jesus, and the mysterious Triune God has entered into us. Once He comes in, the Spirit comes, and the Father and the Son also come. How rich it is now that the Father is in us, the Son is in us, and the Spirit also is in us! Our whole being is now fully taken over by the Triune God. The Triune God has begotten us with Himself and has reconstituted us with His own divine elements. Now we are persons with God, those who have the dispensing of God and are saturated and constituted with God. Hence, we are God-men.

This work of putting the Triune God Himself into us is dispensing. This dispensing is not at all rough; rather, it is very refined and tender. As long as you confess that you are a sinner and believe in the Lord Jesus, this Triune God—the Father, the Son, and the Spirit—will enter into you to be your life and everything. If you are a husband, He will become the love with which you love your wife. If you are a wife, He will become the submission with which you submit to your husband. You can love your wife because of Jesus, and you can submit to your husband because of Jesus. Your humility, gentleness, and patience are all Jesus. Jesus has become your all.

Moreover, through His dispensing within you, you will gradually realize that He is your Head. Before Him you are just like a wife. You will understand that He is your Lord, that only He has the real sovereignty over you. This Triune God who is within you is your life and everything. He is also your Head, your Husband, and your Lord. Moreover, He is your law, the law of the Spirit of life. This law is a tremendous thing. When you see an electric fan turning, you know that there is a law of electricity operating within the electric fan. Electricity is transmitted from the power plant to the house and is then connected to the electric fan. There is also a switch. When you want the fan to turn, you do not need to turn it with a bamboo pole. You only need to turn on the switch; the fan will immediately turn and the cool wind will come.

As a Christian today, do you live the Christian life by "turning the fan with a bamboo pole," or are you "turning on the switch" to allow the fan to turn by itself? Some have prayed much for the Lord to help them and to strengthen them so that they can honor their parents and control their temper. Actually, this kind of prayer is like turning the fan with a bamboo pole. Have you seen that you no longer need to turn the fan with the pole? You need to see that one fact has been accomplished—that the electricity from the power plant has been installed into this house. The electric fan is here. The switch is installed. There is no need for you to do anything else. You only need to turn on the switch, and the fan will turn.

THE OPERATION OF THE TRIUNE GOD
IN THE BELIEVERS

We all have to see that the Triune God is the greatest "electricity." He has been installed in us. Daily He is turning within us in a gentle and fine way. If you contact Him, you will receive the enjoyment. If you ignore Him, you will miss the enjoyment. Very few Christians see this matter. For this reason, we need to ask the Lord to enlighten our understanding and to turn our prayer, so that we will not beg in a poor way anymore. We must praise and thank Him, saying, "Lord, I thank You. You are the law of the Spirit of life, and You have entered into me and remained in me from the first day until now. You have never ceased 'turning.' Lord, praise You, You are still operating in me today in many ways." The Triune God is operating in us daily. This operation is a gentle, refined, and fine dispensing of Himself into all of us.

Tonight we have all eaten some food. When the food enters into us, there is an operation. This operation is our digestion, and this digestion is a law operating in our body. The goal of this law and this operation is to dispense the food bit by bit into our body so that the nutritious elements can be assimilated little by little by our body. The Lord told us clearly in the Gospel of John that He is the bread from heaven. When we eat of Him, there will be an operation within us, enabling us to live by Him (John 6:35, 50-51, 57-58). He also told us that He is the living water. We can drink of Him freely, and He will quench our thirst (John 4:14; 7:37). This also is an operation within us. This operation is His dispensing.

Furthermore, the Lord revealed to us that He is the holy breath, and that we can breathe Him in (John 20:22). This holy breath is the Holy Spirit, who also is the Triune God Himself. He continues to operate and to breathe out, in order that we can continually breathe in and enjoy Him. In this way, there is an organic union between Him and us, a union in which He continually dispenses and we continually receive. In the end, we will lack nothing and will grow in God's life through the increase of His dispensing in us. Today, within every one of us there is such a law. The Triune God is not only our life, but He is also a law that is full of operations in order to continually dispense Himself into us.

Allowing the Law of the Spirit of Life to Operate

Furthermore, Romans 8 tells us that there is another law within us, the law of sin and of death in our flesh. This law causes our body to become weak and to be powerless in carrying out the will of God. It also causes us to be strong and vigorous in doing things that offend God. This law is the law of sin, and it is also the law of death. When these two are added together, we become powerless in doing good and insensitive in doing evil. This law of sin and death is just Satan in our flesh. When man sinned, Satan entered into man. However, when we believe in the Lord, another law enters into us, which is the Triune God coming into us to be our life. This life is not in our flesh but in our spirit. Today, it is very easy for man to sin. As soon as the law of sin and of death works a little, man will spontaneously lie and deceive. Actually, it is not we who are doing these things; it is the law of sin and of death that is doing the work within us. In the same way, within us there is now another law, the law of the Spirit of life. This law is a person, the Triune God. He regulates within us day by day. We do not need to ask Him to help us. As long as He operates, everything will be well. He is not far from us;

He is not high up in heaven. Rather, He is within us. For this reason, we must learn to hand ourselves over to Him and allow Him to be everything to us. He is life within us, and He is also a law within us.

We know that every life has its element, nature, capacity, effect, and form. In addition, every life can propagate. The peach tree has the element of the peach. Based on its element, it has its nature, and this nature produces a capacity. This capacity brings in an effect, which causes the peach tree to bring forth peaches. Moreover, the peaches bear a form, which determines their particular shape. In the same way, we human beings have the element, the nature, the capacity, the effect and the form of the human life. This is true not only with our physical life, but even with our spiritual life. If we allow the Triune God to carry out His refined and gentle dispensing within our tripartite being every day, we will grow and multiply by His growth within us.

(A message given by Brother Witness Lee in Sibu, Malaysia on October 27, 1990)

THE RESULTS OF THE DISPENSING OF THE DIVINE TRINITY AS THE LAW OF THE SPIRIT OF LIFE IN THE BELIEVERS

(1)

OUTLINE AND SCRIPTURE READING

I. **The believers being saved in the life of Christ that they may reign in this life—Rom. 5:10, 17b:**

Romans 5:10
For if, while we were enemies, we were reconciled to God through the death of His Son, much more, having been reconciled, we shall be saved in His life.

Romans 5:17b
...much more those who receive the abundance of grace and of the gift of righteousness shall reign in life through the One, Jesus Christ.

A. **The believers having been reconciled to God through the death of His Son being saved in His life—Rom. 5:10b:**

Romans 5:10b
...having been reconciled, we shall be saved in His life.

1. **To be freed from the law of sin and of death—Rom. 8:2.**

Romans 8:2
For the law of the Spirit of life in Christ

Jesus has freed me from the law of sin and of death.

2. To be saved from the body of this death— Rom. 7:24, cf. Rom. 7:9-13, 21-23.

Romans 7:24

Wretched man that I am! Who will deliver me from the body of this death?

Romans 7:9-13

For I was alive without the law once; but when the commandment came, sin revived, and I died. (10) And the commandment which was unto life, this was found to me to be unto death. (11) For sin, taking occasion through the commandment, deceived me, and through it killed me. (12) So that the law is holy, and the commandment holy and just and good. (13) Did then that which is good become death to me? Certainly not! But sin, that it might appear sin, working death to me through that which is good; that sin through the commandment might become exceedingly sinful.

Romans 7:21-23

I find then the law that, at my willing to do the good, the evil is present with me. (22) For I delight in the law of God according to the inner man, (23) but I see a different law in my members, warring against the law of my mind and making me a captive in the law of sin which is in my members.

3. To be saved from the mortality of the body—Rom. 8:11, 13.

Romans 8:11

But if the Spirit of Him who raised Jesus from among the dead dwells in you, He who raised Christ Jesus from among the dead

will also give life to your mortal bodies
through His Spirit who indwells you.

Romans 8:13
For if you live according to flesh, you are
about to die; but if by the Spirit you put to
death the practices of the body, you will live.

4. To be saved from being common—Rom. 6:19, 22; 12:2a.

Romans 6:19
I speak humanly because of the weakness
of your flesh. For as you presented your
members as slaves to uncleanness and lawlessness unto lawlessness, so now present
your members as slaves to righteousness
unto sanctification.

Romans 6:22
But now, having been freed from sin and
having been enslaved to God, you have your
fruit unto sanctification, and the end eternal
life.

Romans 12:2a
And do not be conformed to this age...

5. To be saved from a low manner of living— Rom. 12:9-21.

Romans 12:9-21
Let love be without hypocrisy. Abhor what is
evil; cleave to what is good. (10) Love one
another warmly in brotherly love, vying with
one another in showing honor, (11) not slothful in zeal, burning in spirit, serving the
Lord as a slave, (12) rejoicing in hope,
enduring in tribulation, persevering in prayer,
(13) communicating to the needs of the
saints, pursuing hospitality. (14) Bless those
who persecute you; bless and do not curse.
(15) Rejoice with those who rejoice, and weep

with those who weep. (16) Be of the same mind toward one another, not minding high things, but being led away to the lowly. Do not be wise in yourselves, (17) repaying no one evil for evil, taking forethought for things honorable in the sight of all men, (18) if possible, as far as it depends on you, living in peace with all men, (19) not avenging yourselves, beloved, but giving place to the wrath of God, for it is written, Vengeance is Mine, I will repay, says the Lord. (20) But if your enemy is hungry, feed him; if he is thirsty give him a drink; for in doing this you will heap coals of fire upon his head. (21) Do not be conquered by the evil, but conquer the evil with the good.

6. To be saved from division—Rom. 16:17.

Romans 16:17

Now I beg you, brothers, keep a watchful eye on those who make divisions and causes of falling contrary to the teaching which you have learned, and turn away from them.

B. The believers reigning in the life of Christ—Rom. 5:17b:

Romans 5:17b

...much more those who receive the abundance of grace and of the gift of righteousness shall reign in life through the One, Jesus Christ.

1. Subduing all the people, events, and things that oppose God's righteousness, holiness, and glory—Rom. 1:17, 7; 3:23.

Romans 1:17

For the righteousness of God is revealed in it out of faith to faith: as it is written, But the just shall live by faith.

Romans 1:7

To all who are in Rome, beloved of God,

called saints: Grace to you and peace from God our Father and the Lord Jesus Christ.

Romans 3:23
For all have sinned and come short of the glory of God;

2. Subduing God's enemy, Satan—Rom. 16:20.

Romans 16:20
Now the God of peace will soon crush Satan under your feet. The grace of our Lord Jesus be with you. Amen.

3. Bringing in God's kingdom—Rom. 14:17.

Romans 14:17
For the kingdom of God is not eating and drinking, but righteousness and peace and joy in the Holy Spirit.

TWO LIVES BECOMING ONE LIFE

In the previous three messages we have seen that the Triune God—the Father, the Son, and the Spirit—has passed through all kinds of processes and has worked Himself into us, the tripartite beings with a spirit, a soul, and a body. For Him to work Himself into us, the main thing is for Him to be our life. Our usual concept is that we need the Lord's redemption and deliverance. We do not have much concept that we need God's life, that is, to have the life of God in addition to our original human life. This does not mean that we will become God and will no longer be man; rather, it means that God will be added into us.

Even if our original human life had not been corrupted, God would not want it. What God wants is not simply His own life but His own life added into our human life. In other words, what God wants is two lives to be joined as one life. In the physical world, the grafting of branches is a simple matter which perfectly symbolizes this union of two lives into one life. For example, here is a peach tree. Its fruit may be small and bitter. Another tree may bear large and sweet peaches. If we graft the branches of the good tree onto the poor peach tree, the union of the two will produce large and sweet fruit. This is the meaning of grafting. It is not a matter of retaining the large and sweet and cutting off the small and bitter. Rather, it is a matter of grafting the large and sweet onto the small and bitter. It is not an exchange or a replacement, but a union. That which is large is grafted onto that which is small, and that which is small is mingled with that which is large. This is the grafted life.

God has no intention for us to stop being man. He has no intention for us to be spirits. God wants us to be God-men, those into whom God has been "grafted." There is no such thing in our concept. In our concept, there is only ourselves, and we consider that we are not too bad. However, we are not good enough; there are still some flaws. As a result, we need some improvement and expect some changes for the better. To change for the better is a human concept. The schools educate people with the hope that man would improve and would be better than before. Although this kind of improvement may superficially seem to work a little, in the end, the person will be worse than before and will have no hope of being improved. God does not want this. He does not want us to have our bright virtue developed, as Confucius said, and to arrive at supreme goodness. He wants us to be filled with God until the living water of life flows out from us like rivers. This is to have the divine life added to the human life, to have God's life grafted into the human life, and to have two lives becoming one life, thus living a mingled living of a God-man.

The highest standard of living for a Christian is to live the mingled life of a God-man. God's purpose is to work Himself into us to the extent that He becomes us and we become Him, that we and He become completely identical in life, nature, and image. This is the pinnacle. This is much higher than being good. Unfortunately, although many of us are saved, we are not very clear about this matter, and do not know what is the real Christian life. We think that the Christian life is merely to have good behavior and to glorify God. But the real meaning of glorifying God is not to do these things, but to express God. We often think that to be humble, patient, and have good works is to glorify God. Actually, our so-called humility, patience, and gentleness do not express God. Rather, they express ourselves.

I fully believe that everyone's condition, including my own, is not quite proper. But thank God, one day we all repented, and we believed in the Lord Jesus. When we called on His name, the holy breath came into us. From that time on, God has been grafted into our life. This Jesus Christ who is in us is the embodiment of the Triune God. Moreover, this embodied Triune God has become a Spirit, who is the compound Spirit of life. He is diverse and all-inclusive. This Spirit is Jesus Christ and is also the Triune God. He is our Redeemer and our Savior as well. When He entered into us, we received another life, the life of God, in addition to our human life. This is called the grafted life. God's life has been grafted into the human life, and the two lives have been joined to become one life. This is like the grafted branches being joined to the tree. Hence, it is not a matter of cultivation or improvement, which has only temporary results. We have God grafted into us. He and we have become one. He is our life, and we are His living. He is our content, and we have become His expression. The Triune God has been processed and has entered into us to be life in our tripartite being, that is, in our spirit, soul, and body. This life is like a law, operating daily in us in a natural, spontaneous, and powerful way. It is like an electric fan, which, though turning slowly, is operating steadily and powerfully. The reason for this is that there is power coming from the power plant. The Triune God can be compared to electricity. He has been processed and has passed through incarnation, human living, crucifixion, death, and resurrection. In resurrection, He has become the life-giving Spirit and has entered into us. This Spirit of life has become a law and is regulating us day by day.

GOING ALONG WITH
THE LAW OF THE SPIRIT OF LIFE

The Triune God as the law of the Spirit of life has been installed into us. The question now is whether or not we are willing to go along and to cooperate with Him. In the Old Testament, the history of Jacob is a type depicting man being full of natural strength. He was born a usurper. Even while he was in his mother's womb, he was fighting with Esau to be the first. He held onto his brother's heel and tried to keep him from coming out first. He was a crafty, calculating, and scheming person. He took over the birthright from his brother by deception, and cheated his father concerning his blessing. Later, under the hand of his uncle, Laban, he took away all the sheep by his tricks. In the end, he even took away his uncle's two daughters and their maids. Yet God had chosen him and had put him in the process of transformation. He disciplined him and dealt with him bit by bit. Once, when he was about to pass over the ford Jabbok, God came in the form of a man to wrestle with him. On that day, it was not God who would not let Jacob go; it was Jacob who would not let God go. God touched the hollow of his thigh, and the hollow of his thigh became out of joint. God changed his name to Israel. From that day on, Jacob was changed. Under God's leading and shepherding, he eventually became God's mature prince, worshipping God and blessing others. The usurper Jacob had been completely subdued by God. He was no longer living by his natural life. Rather, he was living under God's life, having God's life as his life, and living one life with God. What was lived out was no longer Jacob, but Israel. He had subjected his natural life to God's life, and he had allowed God's life to regulate him within continually. As a result, he became the prince of God and God's overcomer.

I see a lot of young people sitting among us here. I would like to say a word to you. I have been following the Lord for over fifty years. I know my Lord. He does not like to deal with man; yet He does want to live out His grafted life from within us. He has grafted Himself into us; now He expects that we would live by this life and would live it out. This requires that we be completely subdued by God's life. You have all been grafted; yet there is still the natural element within you. For this, you need God to touch the hollow of your thigh, so that your life would be dealt with and would no longer be whole, but would be broken and have the genuine transformation. In this way, you will live out God's grafted life.

God's law of the Spirit of life does not move in a rash way within us. Rather, it operates spontaneously and softly. This can be compared to our eating. Within us is a law of digestion that does the work of digestion in us. A little while after the food gets into us, the digestion is completed, and the food becomes our nutrients. It is true that we are not good, but we should not expect to improve quickly. We have to do what *Hymns*, #841, stanza 6, says, "I would cease completely from my efforts vain." We should not struggle or strive anymore. Instead, we should simply hand ourselves over to God's law. We have to know that our natural life is also a law. After Satan entered into man, the natural law within man became distorted. Either we do not love the Lord, or we expect that we can be a "saint." However, we should not expect too much. Instead, we should simply allow the grafted life to grow spontaneously according to its own law of life.

Once I planted a peach tree in my garden. Daily I waited for it to grow. For this reason, I trimmed it daily. But it still would not bear fruit. One day, an expert in gardening visited me. I asked him why my peach tree would not grow. He said, "It is because you have trimmed it too well. If you will stop trimming it, it will bear fruit." It is the same way with God's life in us. I encourage you to love the Lord, to grow, and to be spiritual, but I would not encourage you to be quick. To be quick is not according to the law of life. If you are quick, you will fail through your quickness.

For God to be life in us, everything is steady. He is not limited by time. I am a quick person. In doing everything, I want to be quick. But gradually, I discovered that God as life in me is not like this. He is not quick. After I was saved, I loved the Bible very much. Often I went to the Brethren meetings to meet with them. They knew the truth very well. One day, one of their leading brothers came to me and told me that God is never quick, and that He did everything slowly. God promised that Christ would come, and it was four thousand years later that Christ eventually came. He told Abraham that all the nations of the earth would be blessed because of his seed. It was two thousand years later that this promise was fulfilled. God never does things quickly. There is only one thing that He did quickly, and that is in Luke 15 when He ran out to embrace the prodigal son. In receiving the sinner, God is very quick. In everything else, He is not quick.

BEING SAVED IN THE LIFE OF CHRIST

The Divine Trinity as the law of the Spirit of life is regulating us in a gentle way, dispensing the Triune God into us. As a result, we will be saved in the life of Christ (Rom. 5:10). According to the book of Romans, we are saved from at least six negative things.

Freed from the Law of Sin and Death

First, this law in us saves us bit by bit from the law of sin and death (Rom. 8:2). In our flesh there is a negative law of sin and death. This law causes us to be weak, powerless, and sick, and even to die. This law also causes us to be weakened morally and to sin. As a result, we become powerless in doing good and become insensitive to doing evil. Now, the spontaneous operation of the law of the Spirit of life in my spirit has freed me in everything so that I am delivered from Satan's law of sin and death that dwells in my fallen nature.

Saved from the Body of This Death

Second, the law of the Spirit of life saves us from the body of this death (Rom. 7:24). Our fallen body is called the body of sin. It is also called the body of this death. The body of sin is strong with respect to sinning and transgressing against God, but the body of this death is weak with respect to doing things pleasing to God. Sin lends strength to the fallen body to commit sin, but death causes the corrupted body to be fully weakened and powerless. Hence, whatever we do becomes dead. Even Paul exclaimed at one point: "Who will deliver me from the body of this death?" The answer is in the law of the Spirit of life. This law will not only save us from the law of sin and death, but will also save us from the body of this death.

Saved from the Mortality of the Body

Third, this law of the Spirit of life will save us from the mortality of the body (Rom. 8:11, 13). Due to man's fall, sin with death entered into man's body. As a result, there is mortality with the body. Whatever we do and however we do it, the mortal body always brings death to us. But if we go along with the law of the Spirit of life, spontaneously we will be saved from the mortality of the body.

Saved from Being Common

Fourth, the law of the Spirit of life saves us from being common (Rom. 6:19, 22; 12:2a). In every fallen being, there is a love within his nature for worldliness and for being common. We can never overcome this by our own struggling or striving. Only by living according to the law of the Spirit of life can we be saved gradually from everything common and from the worldly thoughts. I believe more or less you have this experience. The more you fellowship with the Lord, the more your view, taste, and attraction for the common things will be gone.

Saved from a Low Manner of Living

Fifth, the law of the Spirit of life saves us from a low manner of living. Romans 12:9-21 shows us a high standard of living. There is no hatred, only love. There is no complaint, only giving. There is even the love of one's enemy. A low manner of living is one that is jealous of others, that has no love, that remembers only others' shortcomings, and that does not forgive. The law of sin and death causes us to sin, to love the world, to be common, to be defiled, and to be powerless in doing good. The result is that we live a low manner of living. However, the law of the Spirit of life in us is annulling the law of sin and death, sanctifying us, and saving us from a low manner of living to a high standard of living.

Saved from Division

Finally, the law of the Spirit of life saves us from all kinds of division (Rom. 16:17). In Christianity, conflict of human opinions always results in different groups and the establishment of sects. This is division. But if we would allow the law of the Spirit of life to regulate us, this law, through its regulation, will remove the negative element of striving and dividing into parties. To be saved from the law of sin and death, from the body of this death, from the mortality of the body, from being common, from a low manner of living, and from division are all results of the enjoyment of the dispensing of the law of the Spirit of life within us.

REIGNING IN THE LIFE OF CHRIST

On one hand, the law of the Spirit of life saves us in life and delivers us from all negative things. On the other hand, it enables us to reign in life (Rom. 5:17b) and to subdue everything that is contrary to God's righteousness, holiness, and glory. Anything contrary to God's righteousness, holiness, and glory is subdued by the law of the Spirit of life when we go along with it. In other words, this law of the Spirit of life enables us by life to be right, proper, holy, and separated in everything, and to glorify and express God. This is to reign in life.

In addition, this law of the Spirit of life will enable us to subdue God's enemy, Satan, to trample him under our feet (Rom. 16:20), and to bring in God's kingdom, which is righteousness, peace, and joy in the Holy Spirit (Rom. 14:17). If we live in the law of the Spirit of life, we will be proper and right toward others, toward any matters, and toward God, and our relationship with others and with God will be one of peace. In this way, we will have joy in the Holy Spirit; that is, we will have joy before God. This is the reality of the kingdom of God. All these are the results of the continual dispensing and unceasing regulation of the Divine Trinity as the law of the Spirit of life in us.

(A message given by Brother Witness Lee in Sibu, Malaysia on October 28, 1990)

THE RESULTS OF THE DISPENSING OF THE DIVINE TRINITY AS THE LAW OF THE SPIRIT OF LIFE IN THE BELIEVERS

(2)

OUTLINE AND SCRIPTURE READING

II. Every part of the believers being sanctified—Rom. 6:19, 22.

Romans 6:19
I speak humanly because of the weakness of your flesh. For as you presented your members as slaves to uncleanness and lawlessness unto lawlessness, so now present your members as slaves to righteousness unto sanctification.

Romans 6:22
But now, having been freed from sin and having been enslaved to God, you have your fruit unto sanctification, and the end eternal life.

III. The believers' mind being renewed—Rom. 12:2b.

Romans 12:2b
...be transformed by the renewing of the mind, that you may prove by testing what the will of God is, that which is good and well-pleasing and perfect.

IV. Every part of the believers' soul being transformed—Rom. 12:2b.

Romans 12:2b
...be transformed by the renewing of the mind, that you may prove by testing what the will of God is, that which is good and well-pleasing and perfect.

V. The believers being conformed to the image of God's firstborn Son—Rom. 8:29a.

Romans 8:29a
Because whom He foreknew, He also predestinated to be conformed to the image of His Son...

VI. The believers being saturated with the divine glory—the redemption of the body—Rom. 8:30b, 23.

Romans 8:30b
...and whom He justified, these He also glorified.

Romans 8:23
And not only so, but we ourselves also, having the firstfruit of the Spirit, even we ourselves groan in ourselves, eagerly expecting sonship, the redemption of our body.

Prayer: Lord, we worship You from the depths of our being. You have gathered us into Your name again. Here we enjoy Your Spirit and Your word. We fully believe that You will open up to us more of the mysteries in Your word so that we can enter into them, enjoy them, and experience them. Lord, be with us. We need You. Amen!

THE RESULTS OF THE DISPENSING
OF THE DIVINE TRINITY IN THE BELIEVERS

During the past few meetings, I believe we have seen a glorious mystery, which is that the Triune God is working Himself into us to be our life. This life is simply God Himself becoming a law within us with its spontaneous power. Many times we do not know this law and do not feel this law. Nevertheless, it is working within us. Although we have many weaknesses, mistakes, and even failures, we have been preserved and maintained until today because there is such a maintaining and preserving law within us that has kept us here until now.

On the Negative Side

When we read the book of Romans, we can readily find out that its record is from the circumference to the center. This center is the Spirit of life. This Spirit has a law that operates daily in our spirit. Its main function is to free us in many ways. After man became fallen, his whole being was in a fallen condition. He was like a prisoner bound in the bondage of the flesh. Then Christ came. He is the embodiment of the Triune God. He became the Spirit of life and entered into us to be a law, daily regulating us within. This law frees us in Christ Jesus from all of the negative things and saves us from Satan's law of sin and death in our fallen nature and from the body of this death.

When God created man, He created him according to His image and after His likeness. For this reason, the body He created was originally a pure vessel. However, man fell and brought into himself the source of death, Satan. When Satan entered into man, he became the law of sin and death in man's flesh. This law of sin and death not only causes our flesh to have the spontaneous power to sin so that we lose our freedom and become bound by sin, but it also brought in death, which causes us to become powerless in doing good and insensitive in doing evil. As a result, whatever our flesh does becomes death and produces death. Hence, our body becomes the body of this death. But at the time we are saved, the law of the Spirit of life in Christ Jesus frees us from the law of sin and of death and from the body of this death as well.

Furthermore, after man fell, Satan injected himself into the human body. As a result, the human body became corrupted and degenerated into the flesh, bringing mortality, aging, and dying with it. Hence, as far as our fallen body is concerned, we are not living daily, but dying daily. When a person is young, he likes others to celebrate his birthday. But after he becomes old and is in his seventies or eighties, he may not like others to celebrate his birthday anymore. This is like having a deposit of one hundred dollars. If I spend a dollar every year, it means that every year I have one dollar less. There is mortality with our body. This is its fate and its destiny.

Other than the problems we have covered, we have yet another problem, which is that we are common. While we are living on the earth, we are frequently defiled by the filth of the world, and subconsciously we become common. Paul beseeched us in Romans 12:2 that we should not be "conformed to this age." "This age" refers to the present, practical part of the world. It is the part we touch and in which we live. Every age has its particular mode, characteristics, fashions, style, and tide. It is like a mold that molds people into its form. For this reason, what we wear and what we have should be as simple as possible. As long as our needs are met, that is good enough. However, only when the law of the Spirit of life regulates us can we love the Lord and be simple. Therefore, we should fellowship with the Lord and live in the law of the Spirit of life so that our living can be simple and can be freed from the entanglements of the world.

Romans 12 also shows us that a person who lives in the church and in the Body of Christ should have a high standard of living. He should only love, and should not hate. He should only bless, and should not curse. The only way to live this kind of life is by going along with the law of the Spirit of life, allowing this law to regulate and to eliminate from us all the negative elements and low manner of living, so that we can live a life with an excelling standard of morality.

Finally, Romans 16:17 charges us: "Those who make divisions and causes of falling...turn away from them." The two thousand years of Christianity is a history of divisions. Our fallen nature likes to be different from others, to strive to be the first. It does not like to submit to others. All these items are factors for division. Only by being in spirit and going along with the law of the Spirit of life can we receive others from the depth of our heart, and only then can we maintain the oneness of the Body of Christ. Only then can we reckon all the churches to be the same and all the saints to be equally lovable, without any comparison, jealousy, or competition. For this reason, we need to be saved daily to live in the law of the Spirit of life to enjoy the divine dispensing of the Divine Trinity, so that our whole being can be released and can be saved, on the negative side, from the law of sin and of death, from the body of this death, from its mortality, from being common, from a low manner of living, and from division. In this way, we will be saved in the life of Christ and will reign in His life, and we will be delivered from every person, event, or thing that is contrary to God's righteousness, holiness, and glory; we will subdue God's enemy, Satan, and bring in God's kingdom.

On the Positive Side—Sanctifying, Transforming, Conforming, and Redeeming

The dispensing of the Divine Trinity as the law of the Spirit of life in us, the believers, results not only in our being delivered from the negative things and subduing them, but it supplies us positively in our spirit, soul, and body. First, it sanctifies us. This sanctification is not only a positional sanctification, but a dispositional transformation. It comes about through the saturation of our whole being with God's holy nature by the Divine Trinity as the Spirit of life, transforming our natural element into a spiritual element, so that every part of our whole being can be sanctified unto God (Rom. 6:19, 22). Second, our minds are renewed (Rom. 12:2b). The renewing of the mind is the basis of the transformation of the soul. It is the result of our setting our mind on the spirit. While the law of the Spirit of life is dispensing within us, a new essence is added into us, producing a metabolic change which makes us suitable for the practice of the church life. Third, every part of our soul is transformed. Since our mind is the main part of our soul, when our mind is renewed, the will and the emotion, which are the other parts that together with the mind form the soul, are spontaneously renewed also. By this, every part of our soul is transformed (Rom. 12:2b).

Fourth, this law of the Spirit of life becomes a mold within us, conforming us to the image of the firstborn Son of God (Rom. 8:29a). Every life has its structure, shape, and form. As the law of the Spirit of life, the Triune God also has His image, which is the image of the firstborn Son of God. If we walk according to the law of the Spirit of life, He will continually operate in us until we are sanctified, renewed, transformed, and conformed to the image of Christ. Christ is God's firstborn Son, and in the end, we will become His many sons, being exactly the same as the firstborn Son, Christ (Rom. 8:29b).

THE PROCESS OF SANCTIFICATION, RENEWING, TRANSFORMATION, CONFORMATION, AND GLORIFICATION

Finally, our whole being will be saturated by the divine glory, which means that our body will be redeemed (Rom. 8:30b, 23). When Christ comes again, we will receive the full sonship, which is the transfiguration of our body to be the same as His glorious body. Since man fell, his body has degenerated; it can sin, it can commit evil, and it can become tired and sick. The last step of the work of the Triune God as the law of the Spirit of life in us is to redeem our body. According to the principle whereby God regenerates us in our spirit through His Spirit, our body of sin, which is of death and which is mortal, will be fully saturated by the glory of His life and nature. The result is that this body will be transfigured and will become the same as the resurrected and glorious body of His Son. This is the ultimate step of His full salvation.

From this we can see that the Lord's salvation is simply the Lord Himself. He has been processed, having passed through incarnation, human living, crucifixion, and resurrection to become the all-inclusive, compound, life-giving Spirit, entering into us to be a law. This is a tremendous thing. When I was young, I read of the law of the Spirit of life in Romans 8, but I did not understand what it was. Hence, I was not able to say anything about it. After many years, not only have I gained a deeper knowledge, but I have more practical experiences. Now, together with what I have read from others' biographies and the confirmation of their experiences, I am able to speak about this matter.

When the law of the Spirit of life regulates within us, it anoints upon us the divine element of God. This can be compared to painting; we have to apply the paint layer by layer. The more we paint, the more layers of paint there will be. The Triune God is anointing us unceasingly in this way, bringing into us the element of God so that we grow and are transformed. This is what Paul meant when he said that we grow "with the growth of God" (Col. 2:19).

Furthermore, this divine element anointed into us has a sanctifying capacity; it sanctifies us. *Hymns*, #841 says:

> Thou art all my life, Lord,
> In me Thou dost live;
> With Thee all God's fulness
> Thou to me dost give.
> By Thy holy nature
> I am sanctified,
> By Thy resurrection,
> Vict'ry is supplied.

Only the sanctifying nature within God's life-element can sanctify us. This is different from the experiences of the sages in Confucianism, who were products of human cultivation. Our sanctification, however, is a product of the sanctifying work of the life of God.

According to the New Testament, the sanctifying work of the Spirit of life is in three steps. First, at the time we repented and believed, He had sought us out and had separated us from other sinners, convicting us concerning sin (1 Pet. 1:2; John 16:8). Second, at the time of our salvation, He sanctified us positionally (1 Cor. 6:11). Third, while we are seeking to grow in life, He sanctifies us dispositionally (Rom. 6:19, 22). This kind of sanctification is not only positional, separating us from a common and worldly position to one that is of God and for God; it is also a dispositional transformation that saturates our whole being with God's sanctifying nature through Christ as the life-giving Spirit transforming our natural element into the spiritual element.

Now, we need to see in detail how this law of the Spirit of life sanctifies us. First, it renews our mind. The meaning of renewing is to have a new essence added into us, so that we have a metabolic change. After the Spirit of life anoints into us the new element of God, this new element replaces and discharges the old and natural element within us. From our youth when we began to understand things, and throughout the years in which we have worked in society, certain concepts and views have been developed within us. After we were saved, the law of the Spirit of life began to anoint us. This anointing produces an effect, which is to replace our old essence, so that we pick up God's concepts and thoughts, and our view concerning our human life, concerning the world, humanity, and our future destiny is completely changed from man's tradition to God's revelation. This is the renewing of the mind.

In addition, Romans 12:2 says that we should be transformed by the renewing. Not only should our mind be renewed, but our soul must be transformed also. The mind is the main part of the soul. When the mind is renewed, the soul will spontaneously be transformed. Transformation is the inward, metabolic process of God's work. This process spreads God's life and nature into our entire being, especially into our soul, including the emotion, will, judgment, joy, anger, sorrow, and pleasure. God's life and nature then become our new, divine element, which gradually replaces our old, natural element. As a result, we are gradually transformed into His image.

Both the renewing and the transformation are the result of the operation of the Triune God as the law of the Spirit of life in us. If we wait before the Lord all the time, fellowship with Him, cooperate with Him, subject ourselves to Him in everything, and give Him the absolute ground in us, He will anoint us and operate in us daily, adding into us His divine element bit by bit. In this way, we will be sanctified, our minds will be renewed, and our souls will be transformed. Moreover, He will continually transform us until we see the Lord and are changed in image to be perfectly like Christ, that is, conformed to the image of the firstborn Son of God.

What is it to be conformed to the image of God's firstborn Son? It is to pass through death and resurrection and to live out Christ. *Hymns*, #499 says:

> Oh, what a life! Oh, what a peace!
> The Christ who's all within me lives.
> With Him I have been crucified;
> This glorious fact to me He gives.
> Now it's no longer I that live,
> But Christ the Lord within me lives.

This is what it means to be conformed to the image of God's firstborn Son. If we live under the law of the Spirit of life, spontaneously we will live a life of being "no longer I but Christ," a life that passes through death and resurrection and will gradually be conformed to the image of the firstborn Son of God.

In this way, under the anointing of the Spirit of life, we can wait for the day of the redemption of our body. Although we have the divine life in our spirit and are being renewed and transformed in our soul, our body is not fully saturated by God's life yet. Our body is still the flesh. It is still joined to the old creation and is still the body of sin and death. Hence, we have to wait earnestly for Christ the Son of God to come down from heaven. By that time, our body of humiliation will be transfigured and will be conformed to the body of His glory (Phil 3:21). The more we love the Lord and live under the law of the Spirit of life, the more we will be redeemed. Not only will our minds be renewed and our souls transformed, but we will also be conformed to the image of the firstborn Son of God. In the end, our whole being will be saturated with the divine glory. Death will be swallowed up by life, corruption will be swallowed up by incorruption, and our body will be fully redeemed. When Christ appears, we shall appear with Him in glory (Col. 3:4). This is the climax of God's full salvation. It is also the highest result of the dispensing of the law of the Spirit of life in us. Today, we are in this process of sanctification, renewing, transformation, conformation, and glorification.

(A message given by Brother Witness Lee in Sibu, Malaysia on October 28, 1990)

A SUPPLEMENTARY WORD

(2)

The book of Romans indeed occupies a special place. In particular, chapter eight of Romans can be considered the center of the mysteries of the New Testament. The whole New Testament speaks of God's mystery. Today is the age of the church, the age of grace. Actually, it is an age of mysteries. By Revelation 10:7, when the seventh trumpet blows, God's mysteries will be fulfilled. In the Old Testament, before John the Baptist came and before Jesus Christ was born, everything was revealed and was not a mystery. Moses' laws, regulations, ordinances, and the types were all revealed and open. There was no mystery at all. It was not until the conception of the Lord Jesus, that is, the Word becoming flesh, that we have the beginning of the mystery of the New Testament.

The birth of Christ is indeed a mystery. How was He born? Who begat Him? And who was He that was begotten? All these are mysteries. Moreover, even we who have believed in Christ are mysteries. Today we are all sitting here without a special reason, and we are so warm towards each other, singing, shouting, praying, and interceding. Why do we do this? All we can say is that this is a mystery. If you say that you love Christ, how can you love Him if you have never seen Him? This also is a mystery. If you say that Christ as the wonderful One is living in you, what do you mean? All these are mysteries! Hence, the whole of the church age, that is, the age of grace, is an age of mysteries.

LIFE BEING A LAW

Romans 8:2 speaks of the law of the Spirit of life. This life is not the human life; neither is it the animal life nor the plant life. This is the excelling life of God. In the universe, the lowest form of life is the plant life. Higher than that is the animal life. Still higher is the human life, which is the highest form of created life. But above this highest form of created life, there is still God's uncreated life. This life is of the Spirit of life, and this Spirit is a law, which is the law of the Spirit of life.

After the Bible was written, it was translated into all kinds of languages on earth, and now everyone can read it. I have studied the Bible since my youth and have studied it for almost seventy years. In the first forty years, I did not understand the law of the Spirit of life. It did not matter how much I read; I could not understand this. I believe many are like me. I could only say that there is such a thing in the Bible, but in my mind there was no such thing. Moreover, our created mind does not even have the capacity to understand this matter. We read the Bible, and we knew about the phrase, "the law of the Spirit of life," but we did not know what this law of the Spirit of life was. However, we cannot say that there is no such thing simply because we do not understand it. Take our body as an example. Our body is a great mystery to us also. Once I was staying at the house of a saint in Peking. At that time, he was the head of the nursing department of the Peking Hospital, the most famous hospital of the time. He took me to a dinner, and all at the table were senior medical doctors. During the conversation, one doctor said, "We cannot deny that, structurally speaking, the human body is too mysterious. It is so mysterious that we cannot even explain it. It appears that there must be a Sovereign Lord in the universe."

Science is but the discovery of axioms and laws from the phenomena of the universe through scientific methods. Through observing the fact that an apple always falls down and does not go up, Newton discovered the law of gravity. I cannot believe that at the time of Paul, Greek science would be so well developed that man knew what a law was. But Paul discovered a spontaneous and naturally existing law, which he called the law of the Spirit of life. Every time you say: "Lord Jesus, I believe in You; I love You; I receive You," you may not notice anything. But something happens within you. Something is added into you. It is Jesus; it is Christ; it is the Holy Spirit; it is also God. Paul said that it is a life and a law. This law has been recorded in the Bible for a long time, and seeking Christians have read it many times, but seldom can one hear anyone speaking about it. Because the light of the Lord's truth among us has been shining brighter and brighter, we are clearer and clearer concerning this matter. About fifteen years ago, I began to speak to people about the law of the Spirit of life.

ALL HUMAN LAWS

Today is the age of science, and every one of us knows what a law is. It is a natural, instinctive, and spontaneous power. The law of the Spirit of life as described by Paul is of the same principle. It exists by itself, and it operates in us spontaneously and functions instinctively. Paul said in Romans 6 that God gave the law to expose the real condition of man. Once man is placed under God's law, he will suffer the condemnation of the law. However, everyone who fears God wants to be free from sin, to strive to keep God's law, and to please God. Even Paul himself was no exception. While he was trying his best to keep God's law and to avoid sin and evil, he discovered that in his members there was another law which was warring against his law of trying to do good. In the end, he did what he did not want to do, and he could not do what he wanted to do. He said, "But if what I do not will, this I do, it is no longer I that do it but sin that dwells in me" (Rom. 7:20). It seems as if Paul was putting off his responsibility when he spoke this word. He said that in his members, that is, in his flesh, there was another law, the law of sin and of death, which always warred against the law of good in his mind and which captured him, causing him to do that which he would not do. All the time he was defeated by this law, and he was indeed a wretched man.

The Chinese philosophers have also discovered that with man there is a battle between reason and lust. In other words, within man there is one part that is reasonable. But there is another part that has evil lusts and that fights with reason all the time. Reason is always overcome by lust. Take the example of the game of mahjong. Some who are addicted to it can play that game for three days and three nights. The more they play it, the more addicted they become. They can even go on without eating or sleeping, and there is nothing they can do to control themselves. This is like what Paul said in Romans 7, that in our flesh dwells a lust or an evil that we cannot overcome or understand. From this, we can see that what the Chinese philosophers said is very much the same as what Paul said.

Therefore, we can see that there is the law of God outside of us exposing our true condition. There is also the law of good created by God within our humanity which demands that we please God. In addition, in our fallen flesh, there is the law of sin and of death, which wars with the law of good in our mind and which captures us. The law of God outside of us is objective, and the law of good as well as the law of sin and death within us are subjective. These two within us always war with each other. This is why Paul cried: "Wretched man that I am! Who will deliver me from the body of this death?" In the end, he had a greater and more wonderful discovery. He said: "Thanks be to God through Jesus Christ our Lord," through whom he found his deliverance.

THE DISCOVERY OF
THE LAW OF THE SPIRIT OF LIFE

Paul discovered that after a man is saved, the Triune God comes in. When the Triune God comes in, He comes in to be man's life. This life is a law, which is the law of the Spirit of life. It is not in man's mind nor is it in man's flesh; rather, it is in man's spirit. In the beginning when God created man, He created for him not only a soul and a body, but also a spirit within his deepest part. The spirit is the highest and most excelling part of man. Paul discovered that when he believed into the Lord Jesus, the Triune God entered into his spirit to be his life. This life in his spirit was a law. Whenever he loved the Lord, prayed to Him, and drew near to Him, this law operated automatically. We who have the same experience can testify to this fact. Anytime and anywhere, as long as we draw near to God a little and call on Him, within the deepest part of our being there will rise up a desire to please God and to be one with Him.

Every genuine believer will discover that every time he draws near to God, deep within him there is a spontaneous power that enables him to honor his parents and to be humble and accommodating. He does not have to grit his teeth to do it. Rather, it is a spontaneous expression. Formerly, we liked to fight to win. Now the pride and the repugnance are gone; we do not fight with others any longer. This is not something that originates from us. Rather, it comes from the spontaneous law within us that supplies us with life, wisdom, and power. Hence, we do not have to make up our mind to be good and to please God. We need only to draw near to God and to fellowship with Him. Spontaneously, within us there will be a life-power that enables us to live a life that pleases God. This can be compared to the digestion in the human body. Once food comes into us, there is no need for us to struggle and to strive. Spontaneously, a law will be there doing the work of digestion gently and slowly, making the food our nutrients and our constitution.

THE OPERATION OF
THE LAW OF THE SPIRIT OF LIFE

Romans 8:1-13 is one section. It speaks of the law of the Spirit of life. Verses 14 to 30 are another section. It speaks of the need for the children of God to go through suffering before they can be glorified and can become legal heirs. This is why it is hard for us to avoid sufferings and groanings. Not only are we ourselves groaning, but the whole creation is groaning as well. It and we are all travailing in pain and are expecting the revelation of the sons of God. The whole universe is a travailing woman, working to produce a corporate son. This corporate son is Jesus Christ and His many brothers. He is the Firstborn, and His many brothers are the many sons. One day God's many sons will be revealed. Then all the creation of the whole universe will enjoy complete freedom. When the sons of God are glorified, they will become God's heirs to inherit God's inheritance. That will be the time of the millennium, the time of the restoration of all things.

Today, we are in this process of travailing. Not only does the whole creation groan; even we who have the Spirit within us as the firstfruit of the Spirit also groan. This is because we have not yet entered into the freedom of the glory of the children of God. Our bodies are not yet redeemed, and we have not yet received the full sonship. We are waiting for the Lord's return, when our bodies will be transfigured and redeemed. At that time our whole being will enter into glory and will be delivered from the slavery of corruption to enjoy the freedom of the glory of the children of God.

In verse 26 Paul said again: "And in like manner the Spirit also joins in to help us in our weakness; for we do not know for what we should pray as is fitting, but the Spirit Himself intercedes for us with groanings which cannot be uttered." From this we can see that the way the Spirit joins in to help us in our weakness is not rough but fine. It is even in the way of a groaning. Today, although we have the Spirit in us as the firstfruit for our foretaste, the fact that we are yet in the process of entering into glory and into full freedom makes it unavoidable for us to often groan. When we are weak, helpless, and powerless, we can only groan. When we groan, God also groans. While we are groaning, the Spirit who is the law within us spontaneously helps us and groans with us.

In verse 23 it is our groaning. In verse 26 it is the Spirit's groaning. The Spirit is higher than all creatures; He is omnipresent and omnipotent, and He is very resourceful. Yet when we groan, He groans with us. In our weakness, He joins in to help us. He is the companion in our weakness and for our sake becomes the same as we are. This proves that the One who comes as the law of the Spirit of life regulates us in a very fine way. He groans when we groan. Sometimes, you have some definite burden and problem that you bring to the Lord. You want to pray, but you cannot utter a prayer. You do not know what you should say, and you can only groan. At such times, the Spirit groans within you also. When we are weak, He joins us in our weakness. Actually, He is not a weak One. But for our sake, He joins in and shares our burden.

OBEYING THE LAW OF THE SPIRIT OF LIFE

Furthermore, the moving and operation of the law of the Spirit of life within us is such that it is difficult to tell whether it is our own moving, or His moving in us. Actually, to our realization, the operation of the law of the Spirit within us is just like our own moving. Whenever we feel that we are weak, depressed, and backsliding, we can pray and draw near to the Lord, and spontaneously there will be an operation which revives us. This is the operation of the gentle indwelling law of the Spirit. We may feel that it comes from ourselves and find it very difficult to differentiate one from the other. But we have to know that whatever comes in the way of the Spirit comes out of the law.

The most precious thing for a Christian to have is the law of this Spirit. Hence, we have to pay attention to this law, to cherish the inward feeling of this law, and to live according to the spontaneous operation of this law within us. In this way, we will surely see a wonderful result. I hope that you will all learn to know this law and to experience this law. Do not mistake it as your own moving simply because He operates in a gentle and fine way. This moving is not something out of us. Rather, it is the operation of the Triune God. We need to cooperate with this law and to go along with its operation within us so that God's element can increase within us and we can grow continually in His life.

(A message given by Brother Witness Lee in Sibu, Malaysia on October 29, 1990)

CHAPTER SEVEN

THE GOAL OF THE DISPENSING OF THE DIVINE TRINITY IN THE BELIEVERS

OUTLINE AND SCRIPTURE READING

I. **To build up the many members into the Body of Christ:**

A. **Coordinating together and functioning according to the measure of each one part— Rom. 12:3-8.**

Romans 12:3-8

For I say through the grace given to me to every one among you, not to think more highly of himself than he ought to think, but to think so as to be sober-minded, as God has allotted to each a measure of faith. (4) For as in one body we have many members, and all the members do not have the same function, (5) so we, being many, are one body in Christ, and severally members one of another. (6) And having gifts that differ according to the grace given to us, let us exercise them accordingly: whether prophecy, according to the proportion of faith; (7) or service, in the service; or he who teaches, in teaching; (8) or he who exhorts, in exhortation; he who gives, in simplicity; he who leads, in diligence; he who shows mercy, in cheerfulness.

B. **Living a life of virtues of the highest standard—Rom. 12:9-21.**

Romans 12:9-21

Let love be without hypocrisy. Abhor what is evil; cleave to what is good. (10) Love one another warmly in brotherly love, vying with one another in showing honor, (11) not slothful in zeal, burning in spirit, serving the Lord as a slave, (12) rejoicing in hope, enduring in tribulation, persevering in prayer, (13) communicating to the needs of the saints, pursuing hospitality. (14) Bless those who persecute you; bless and do not curse. (15) Rejoice with those who rejoice, and weep with those who weep. (16) Be of the same mind toward one another, not minding high things, but being led away to the lowly. Do not be wise in yourselves, (17) repaying no one evil for evil, taking forethought for things honorable in the sight of all men, (18) if possible, as far as it depends on you, living in peace with all men, (19) not avenging yourselves, beloved, but giving place to the wrath of God, for it is written, Vengeance is Mine, I will repay, says the Lord. (20) But if your enemy is hungry, feed him; if he is thirsty give him a drink; for in doing this you will heap coals of fire upon his head. (21) Do not be conquered by the evil, but conquer the evil with the good.

II. That the unique Body of Christ may be expressed in the local churches in every place:

A. All the churches needing:

1. To receive all genuine believers unconditionally according to the way God and Christ receive them—Rom. 14:1-3; 15:7.

Romans 14:1-3

Now him who is weak in faith receive, not with a view to passing judgment on reasonings. (2) One believes that he may eat all things, but he who is weak eats vegetables. (3) Let not him who eats despise him who does not eat, and let not him who does not eat judge him who eats, for God has received him.

Romans 15:7
Wherefore receive one another, as Christ also received us to the glory of God.

2. **To treat all genuine believers according to Christ—Rom. 15:5.**

Romans 15:5
Now the God of endurance and encouragement grant you to be likeminded one toward another according to Christ Jesus.

3. **To walk according to love—Rom. 14:15.**

Romans 14:15
But if because of food your brother is grieved, you no longer walk according to love. Do not destroy by your food that man for whom Christ died.

4. **To live under the light of the judgment-seat of God—Rom. 14:10b.**

Romans 14:10b
...for we shall all stand before the judgment-seat of God.

5. **To live a life of the kingdom of God—Rom. 14:17.**

Romans 14:17
For the kingdom of God is not eating and drinking, but righteousness and peace and joy in the Holy Spirit.

6. **All the churches and all the saints on the whole earth living in one universal fellowship—Rom. 16:1-27.**

Romans 16:1-27
I commend to you our sister Phoebe, who is a deaconess of the church which is at Cenchrea, (2) that you may receive her in the Lord in a manner worthy of the saints and stand by her in whatever she may have need

of you; for she has been a patroness of many and of myself as well. (3) Greet Prisca and Aquila, my fellow workers in Christ Jesus, (4) who risked their own necks for my life, to whom not only I give thanks, but also all the churches of the nations; (5) and greet the church in their house. Greet Epaenetus, my beloved, who is the firstfruit of Asia unto Christ. (6) Greet Mary, who has labored for us. (7) Greet Andronicus and Junia, my kinsmen and my fellow prisoners, who are notable among the apostles, who also were in Christ before me. (8) Greet Ampliatus, my beloved in the Lord. (9) Greet Urbanus, our fellow worker in Christ, and Stachys, my beloved. (10) Greet Apelles, approved in Christ. Greet those who belong to Aristobulus. (11) Greet Herodion, my kinsman. Greet those belonging to Narcissus, who are in the Lord. (12) Greet Tryphaena and Tryphosa, who labor in the Lord. Greet Persis, the beloved, who has labored much in the Lord. (13) Greet Rufus, chosen in the Lord, and his mother and mine. (14) Greet Asyncritus, Phlegon, Hermas, Patrobas, Hermes, and the brothers with them. (15) Greet Philologus, and Julia, Nereus and his sister, and Olympas, and all the saints with them. (16) Greet one another with a holy kiss. The churches of Christ greet you. (17) Now I beg you, brothers, keep a watchful eye on those who make divisions and causes of falling contrary to the teaching which you have learned, and turn away from them. (18) For such men do not serve as slaves our Lord Christ, but their own appetites; and by smooth and flattering speech deceive the hearts of the simple. (19) For the report of your obedience has reached to all; therefore I rejoice over you, but I want you to be wise to what is good and pure to what is evil. (20) Now the God of peace will soon crush Satan under your feet. The grace of our Lord Jesus be with you. Amen. (21) Timothy, my fellow worker, and Lucius and Jason and Sosipater, my kinsmen, greet you. (22) I, Tertius, who write this epistle, greet you in the Lord. (23) Gaius, my host, and of the whole church, greets you. Erastus, the city-treasurer, greets you, and Quartus, the brother. (25) Now to Him who is of power to establish you according to my gospel and the preaching of Jesus Christ, according to the revelation of the mystery, which has been kept in silence in times eternal, (26) but now has been manifested, and by the Scriptures of the prophets, according to the command of the eternal God, has been made known to all the nations unto obedience of faith, (27) to the only wise God through Jesus Christ be the glory forever and ever! Amen.

7. **To turn away from those who cause divisions—Rom. 16:17.**

Romans 16:17

Now I beg you, brothers, keep a watchful eye on those who make divisions and causes of falling contrary to the teaching which you have learned, and turn away from them.

B. The results:

1. **Crushing Satan under our feet—Rom. 16:20a.**

Romans 16:20a

Now the God of peace will soon crush Satan under your feet...

2. **Enjoying the grace of Christ and the peace of God—Rom. 16:20.**

Romans 16:20
Now the God of peace will soon crush Satan under your feet. The grace of our Lord Jesus be with you. Amen.

3. Giving glory to the only wise God—Rom. 16:25-27.

Romans 16:25-27
Now to Him who is of power to establish you according to my gospel and the preaching of Jesus Christ, according to the revelation of the mystery, which has been kept in silence in times eternal, (26) but now has been manifested, and by the Scriptures of the prophets, according to the command of the eternal God, has been made known to all the nations unto obedience of faith, (27) to the only wise God through Jesus Christ be the glory forever and ever! Amen.

THE STRUCTURE OF THE BOOK OF ROMANS

In order to understand the book of Romans, we must first know the structure of this book. We know that the most important part of a man's face is his eyes. Many Bible scholars acknowledge the book of Romans as the eyes of the New Testament. This book as the eyes of the New Testament was written by Paul in Corinth. It speaks of God's mysterious economy, His dispensing, and its results.

Not long after Paul wrote 1 and 2 Corinthians in Ephesus, he went to the problem-ridden church in Corinth. I believe that while he was there, confronted with all the practical situations, he had some observations and ideas. This became the structure from which he wrote the book of Romans. His intention was to show God's people the mysterious economy of God, how His dispensing produced redemption, and how from this redemption, through His continual dispensing, the chosen tripartite man would be fully saturated by His divine element. Such ones would not only have God's life through regeneration, but would also be sanctified, renewed, transformed, and even conformed in their whole being from inside to outside, from their spirit through their soul to their body, to the image of God's firstborn Son, living a life of death and resurrection. Furthermore, they would be coordinated and built up together as a corporate vessel to be the Body of Christ, His counterpart that would be expressed on earth in different localities. Although they would live in different places, they would not be separated, but would be constituted as the unique Body of Christ, having one universal fellowship and becoming the full expression of Christ. This is the structure of Romans.

The apostle Paul saw that the ultimate goal of God's purpose is to build up together the tripartite men who have been redeemed and who possess His life to be His sons into a Body for His corporate expression on earth. In other words, God wants to gain sons from among the sinners, so that they can be constituted the Body of Christ for the expression of Christ. This expression appears on earth in individual localities, each unit being determined by the administrative boundaries. Although they appear in different places, they are not separate, and although they are local, they are still part of the unique universal Body of Christ. When Paul wrote this book, this thought was deeply planted in his heart and spirit. Hence, with that as the foundation, Paul wrote this book and sent it to the church in Rome.

Romans 1 begins clearly and definitely with the gospel of God. The gospel of God is the subject of Romans; it begins from God's creation and proves God's existence by the heaven and the earth. However, the created man did not worship God according to His eternal power and divinity which are manifested in the universe. On the contrary, man sinned and offended God, so that he was condemned by God's righteous law. For this, God accomplished redemption in Christ for the fallen sinners, and through faith on the sinners' part redeemed them back one by one. Through incarnation, human living, and crucifixion, God died for man and redeemed him, overcoming Satan, and in resurrection became the life-giving Spirit, entering into those who believe in Him and call on Him to be their life and everything. This is the gospel of God's salvation.

This gospel has been preached to the ends of the earth. All those that hear this, who believe and call on the name of the Lord Jesus, will have the pneumatic Christ enter into them to regenerate their spirit. From that time on, these regenerated ones are able to breathe in God and receive Him; they can take in God, and Christ, who also is the life-giving Spirit, as the breath of life; they can also take in the Spirit of life as the living water, drinking Him for the quenching of their thirst. Moreover, they can eat the Lord as the heavenly spiritual food through the word of the Bible. Through this kind of breathing, drinking, and eating of the Lord, the life-giving Spirit can continue to do the dispensing work within the believers. This dispensing is like the anointing; it anoints repeatedly, layer by layer, God's divine element and His sanctifying and glorious life-essence into those who believe in Him and enjoy Him. In this way, these ones will abide in Him, and the Lord will abide in them. There will be no barrier between them and the Lord. They will receive more of the Lord's fatness and enjoy His divine element, and they will grow with the increase of God within them. In the end, they will not only be regenerated, but will also be sanctified, renewed, and transformed. Throughout this process, they will experience Christ's death and resurrection and will be conformed to the image of Christ, the firstborn Son of God. Finally, all these ones who believe in the Lord and enjoy Him become a corporate vessel in the universe, constituted the Body of Christ to be the expression of Christ in every locality for the fulfillment of God's desire. This is what is revealed in Romans chapters one to sixteen.

In the previous few messages, we have covered the main points prior to chapter twelve. In this message, we will consider the content of four chapters: twelve, fourteen, fifteen, and sixteen. Romans 12 shows us that we who have received Christ and enjoy Him are the members of Christ, being coordinated and built up together, and constituted the Body of Christ. The other three chapters show us that, on the one hand, this unique Body of Christ is expressed in localities city by city in various countries on earth as the local churches; on the other hand, because the fellowship of this Body is universal, these local churches are still one. In this way, they will give glory to the one wise God.

In the previous messages, we have seen the divine dispensing of the Divine Trinity, and we have seen the results of this divine dispensing. Now we want to consider the goal of this dispensing. The goal of the dispensing of the Divine Trinity within the believers is simply to have a Body expressed as the many local churches. Although there are many churches, there is nevertheless one Body. On the one hand, we have the Body of Christ, which is universal. On the other hand, the Body is expressed in various localities as local churches. Universally speaking, there is one Body. Locally speaking, there are many local churches.

BUILDING UP THE MANY MEMBERS
INTO THE BODY OF CHRIST

Coordinating Together and Functioning
according to the Measure of Each One Part

First, the goal of God's dispensing is to build up the many

members into the Body of Christ. In the Body of Christ, all the members coordinate together and function according to the measure of each one part (Rom. 12:3-8). Paul said in Romans 12:3, "For I say through the grace given to me to every one among you, not to think more highly of himself than he ought to think, but to think so as to be sober-minded, as God has allotted to each a measure of faith." Sober-mindedness here means to not be careless or foolish, to consider things properly, without being too much or too little. In the coordination of the Body, we have to consider ourselves soberly. We must not only consider ourselves from our own standpoint, but must know ourselves as we are in the Body of Christ. If God has set you in the Body of Christ as a little finger, and if you have the view of the Body, you will accept it with gladness. This is to be sober-minded.

Following this, verses 4 and 5 say: "For as in one body we have many members, and all the members do not have the same function, so we, being many, are one body in Christ, and severally members one of another." Hence, all of us have to know what part we are in the Body and what function we have (vv. 6-8). We must also be sober-minded, so that we can coordinate with others in the church and can be built up together. Many times, problems in the church arise because believers consider others and make judgments based on the natural view. For this reason, we have to be delivered from ourselves and from the natural man, so that our minds can be sober and can make judgments accurately. In this way, we can stand in the proper position and can happily coordinate to be built up with others. We will function according to our own measure, and we will neither overstep others nor underestimate ourselves. In this way, the Body will be built up.

Living a Life of Virtues of the Highest Standard

Romans 12:9-11 shows us a life of the highest standard of virtues in the Body. This portion shows us that the life of the highest standard of virtues exceeds the requirement of human ethics and morality. This is the life that we Christians should live in the church before men. Only by this can we coordinate and be built up properly and suitably with others as one.

I believe many of you here are married. Can you tell me of one couple who never argues? If arguments are unavoidable even between husbands and wives, how can we avoid them among the brothers and sisters in the church? Paul said in Philippians 2:14, "Do all things without murmurings and reasonings." Murmurings are from the emotion and come mainly from the sisters. Reasonings are from the mind and come mainly from the brothers. Both of these things frustrate us, so that we cannot fully experience and enjoy Christ. Whether it is the murmuring of the sisters or the reasoning of the brothers, both are the flesh that has not been dealt with and that has not passed through the cross. If we are persons who have passed through the cross, it will be no longer we who live, but Christ living in us. When we die and live with Christ in this way, we will be conformed to the image of the firstborn Son of God and will become persons who have passed through death and resurrection. In this way, the church life will be full of peace and joy.

THAT THE UNIQUE BODY OF CHRIST MAY BE EXPRESSED THROUGH THE VARIOUS LOCAL CHURCHES

Receiving All Genuine Believers Unconditionally according to the Way God and Christ Receive Them

When we live a life with the highest virtues, the church will become a coordinated and built-up Body that is expressed in all the localities. Hence, chapter fourteen shows us the unique Body of Christ expressed in all the local churches. For this reason, all the churches have to receive all genuine believers unconditionally, according to the way God and Christ receive them (Rom. 14:1-3; 15:7), for the practice of the Body life. We have to learn the practical lesson of receiving the believers. Here Paul used eating and the keeping of the Sabbath as examples. He said that some are still keeping the Sabbath, and others are still eating according to the ceremony of cleansing. But as long as they have all believed in the Lord, we have to receive them. Although those who keep the Sabbath are wrong, God still receives them. Although the

Jewish believers may keep the ceremonies of the Old Testament, God receives them also. God's receiving is not based on the question of the Sabbath or the ordinances of eating, but on man's believing in Jesus Christ the Son of God. Our receiving of the believers is based on God's receiving of them. Hence, all the churches have to receive them also. When we receive in this way, according to God instead of according to doctrine or methods, we maintain the oneness of the Body of Christ.

Treating All Genuine Believers according to Christ

After receiving them, we still have to treat all genuinely saved believers according to Christ. Romans 15:5 says: "Now the God of endurance and encouragement grant you to be likeminded one toward another according to Christ Jesus." God has Christ Jesus as the standard in the church life. In the church life, everything must be according to Him, instead of according to doctrines and knowledge. No matter how different others are from us in doctrinal views or religious practices, we must learn to treat them according to Christ. We must treat them not only according to Christ's mind, but according to Christ Himself. In this way we will be able to think the same thing.

Walking according to Love

In 14:15 Paul said, "But if because of food your brother is grieved, you no longer walk according to love." No matter how different others are from us in concept or practice, we should not criticize or judge them. Otherwise, we are not walking according to love, and we will be putting a stumbling block before others, thus causing others to stumble, and damaging the Body life.

Living in the Light of God's Judgment-Seat

Romans 14:10 also tells us that we should not judge others in anything, because "we shall all stand before the judgment-seat of God." One day, God's judgment-seat will reveal all our deeds and actions. Hence, today, we have to live and work under the light of God's judgment-seat in everything.

Living Out the Life of God's Kingdom

Today, in the Lord's recovery, the most important thing is to keep the oneness of the Body of Christ. This oneness is different from being united. Being united means that a number of people are joined together. But oneness is to have only one person, who is the pneumatic Christ Himself living in us, so that we can do everything according to God and Christ and can be built up in the Body to live out the life of God's kingdom. Romans 14:17 says: "For the kingdom of God is not eating and drinking, but righteousness and peace and joy in the Holy Spirit." God's kingdom is the sphere for God to exercise His authority and where God expresses His glory and accomplishes His will. It is not a matter of eating and drinking, but righteousness, peace, and joy in the Holy Spirit. We who live in God's kingdom should be right and proper toward men, toward all things, and toward God. We should be without mistakes, prejudices, or deviations. In this way, we will have peace as the proper relationship between us and others and between us and God. There will be no criticisms or disputes. If we are right toward man and God, and we are at peace with all men, we will have joy in the Holy Spirit. In this way, we will have the reality of the kingdom life.

All the Churches and All the Saints
on the Whole Earth Living in
One Universal Fellowship

From the whole chapter of Romans 16 we can see that all the churches and all the saints on the whole earth live in one universal fellowship (vv. 1-27). When Paul wrote the book of Romans, Corinth and Rome were geographically far apart from one another. The means of communication were not advanced. Yet in Paul's numerous greetings in verses 1 through 27 he mentioned many names. Although he was never in Rome, there were many people in Rome who knew him. This shows that although the churches then appeared in different localities, and there were saints all over the earth, they were still living in the one fellowship of the Body. In whatever nation or land the churches were found, they were still one Body. All the saints are members of this Body, and they live in the oneness of this Body of Christ.

Turning Away from Those Who Cause Division

In 16:17 Paul said: "Now I beg you, brothers, keep a watchful eye on those who make divisions and causes of falling contrary to the teaching which you have learned, and turn away from them." In chapter fourteen, in the matter of receiving those with different doctrines and practices, Paul was very broad and flexible. But here, he resolutely charged us to turn away from those who hold dissenting opinions and who make divisions and causes of falling. Both aspects are for the maintaining of the oneness of the Body of Christ, so that we can live the proper church life.

THE RESULTS

When we live in the oneness of the Body of Christ and express this Body in the various local churches, the result will be: (1) God's crushing of Satan under our feet (Rom. 16:20a), (2) our enjoying the grace of Christ and the peace of God (Rom. 16:20b), and (3) the giving of glory to the only wise God (Rom. 16:25-27). This is the peak of our church life. No matter how many saints or local churches there are on earth, in the various places we all give glory to the only wise God. This God is the One who has given Jesus Christ to us according to the revelation of the mystery which has been kept in silence in times eternal, who also is the One who has saved us, regenerated us, and through His divine dispensing is continually sanctifying, renewing, and transforming us, and who will eventually glorify us and conform us to the image of God's firstborn Son, bringing us into glory. Now all of us are in this Body of Christ, glorifying our God to eternity.

(A message given by Brother Witness Lee in Sibu, Malaysia on October 29, 1990)

SECTION III

The Divine Dispensing of the All-inclusive Christ and Its Functions

CHAPTER EIGHT

THE DIVINE DISPENSING
OF THE ALL-INCLUSIVE CHRIST
IN SUPPLYING AND SUSTAINING
THE BELIEVERS

OUTLINE AND SCRIPTURE READING

I. **The all-inclusive Christ being the divine dispensing as the common portion from God to the believers, supplying to them the riches of God in Christ:**

   A. **Being enjoyed by the believers together— 1 Cor. 1:2b.**

   1 Corinthians 1:2b
   ...with all those who call upon the name of our Lord Jesus Christ in every place, theirs and ours.

   B. **Being what God has called the believers into—1 Cor. 1:9.**

   1 Corinthians 1:9
   God is faithful, through whom you were called into the fellowship of His Son, Jesus Christ our Lord.

II. **The all-inclusive Christ being the divine dispensing as the power from God to the believers, supplying and sustaining them in what they are and what they do—1 Cor. 1:24a:**

   1 Corinthians 1:24a
   But to those who are called, both Jews and Greeks...

A. Being with a dynamic power.

B. Strengthening the believers.

III. The all-inclusive Christ being the divine dispensing as the wisdom from God to the believers, sustaining them in the divine economy and plan—1 Cor. 1:24b, 30:

1 Corinthians 1:24b
...Christ, God's power and God's wisdom.

1 Corinthians 1:30
But of Him you are in Christ Jesus, who became wisdom to us from God: both righteousness and sanctification and redemption.

A. Being with counsel.

B. Affording the saints the strategies.

IV. The all-inclusive Christ being the divine dispensing as the righteousness from God to the believers, supplying to them the righteous way of God—1 Cor. 1:30:

1 Corinthians 1:30
But of Him you are in Christ Jesus, who became wisdom to us from God: both righteousness and sanctification and redemption.

A. In procedures and methods.

B. That the believers may be perfectly righteous and right toward God, toward men, and toward all things.

V. The all-inclusive Christ being the divine dispensing as the sanctification from God to the believers, supplying to them God's sanctifying nature—1 Cor. 1:30:

1 Corinthians 1:30
But of Him you are in Christ Jesus, who became wisdom to us from God: both righteousness and sanctification and redemption.

A. In position and nature.

B. **That the believers' spirit, soul, and body may be fully sanctified.**

VI. **The all-inclusive Christ being the divine dispensing as the redemption from God to the believers, supplying to them daily the divine glory which manifests God—1 Cor. 1:30:**

1 Corinthians 1:30
But of Him you are in Christ Jesus, who became wisdom to us from God: both righteousness and sanctification and redemption.

A. **Not only for the believers' life and walk today;**

B. **But for their future redemption of the body, that their whole being may enter God's glory and may express God's glory and radiance forever.**

Prayer: Lord, we worship You from our depths, that You have gathered us once again into Your name. Lord, we believe You are with us, that Your Spirit is here, and that Your word is opened up to us. Lord, we thank You that in this dark age, we have Your bright holy word in our hands, as a lamp that shines in a dark place. We fully believe that You will release Yourself from Your word tonight. Lord, we want to be fully open to You. May Your Spirit move freely in this meeting. Lord, fill us all, and transfuse Your desire and Your word into us and into our mouth. May our speaking be Your speaking, and may You speak in our speaking. Lord, deliver us from wasted and idle words, so that we can speak purely about You, about Your glory, Your person, what You are, and what You have done, and may all of us gain something from You. Lord, cover all of us with Your victorious blood. Oppose for us all the powers of darkness. May glory be to You and blessing be to the saints. Amen.

During the last ten years, from 1980 until now, the Lord's leading among us has gradually opened up to us in one specific direction the mysteries in the Bible. This direction is the divine economy. With this divine economy, there is a divine dispensing. The word "economy" was used especially by Paul in his Epistles (Eph. 1:10; 3:9; 1 Cor. 9:17; 1 Tim. 1:4). The word means a plan, an arrangement, and a purpose. God's economy, plan, arrangement, and purpose is to dispense Himself into His chosen, created, and redeemed people. When we repent and believe in the Lord, God redeems, justifies, and regenerates us. This first step of regeneration, by which God enters into our spirit, is the beginning of God's dispensing into us. Hence, regeneration is the beginning of the divine dispensing of the divine economy. Through this dispensing, the complete God is dispensed into millions of people. He is in you and at the same time is in me. He is in all of those who have believed in the Lord. Throughout the ages, millions of believers have had this same God within them. He has dispensed Himself to us, yet He Himself is not divided. He is complete in every one of us who has believed. This One is complete, yet He is distributed to everyone, and everyone has a part in Him.

This is like a house that has been completed, whose power lines have been installed. When it is connected to the power source, electricity comes. From that time on, the electricity stored in the power station is continually distributed into the house, and all the electric appliances are able to function. The operation of all the appliances depends on the distribution of the power station. Once the electricity stops, everything loses its function. Today, in this universe, there is a tremendous thing. Our God is like electricity. One day He installed Himself from the heavenly power station into us, the believers. During the past ten years, among us the Lord has shown us continually that God has a mysterious economy, which is to dispense Himself as a complete Being into every one of us. When we call on the name of the Lord, believe, and are baptized, God is transmitted into us. The Triune God has dispensed Himself into us. Within us, such a wonderful dispensing has taken place.

In the previous messages, we have seen God's dispensing from the Gospel of John and from the book of Romans respectively. Later, we will consider God's dispensing from the book of Ephesians. Now we will consider God's dispensing from 1 and 2 Corinthians.

BEING THE DIVINE DISPENSING
AS THE COMMON PORTION
FROM GOD TO THE BELIEVERS

Through the divine dispensing, the all-inclusive Christ becomes the common portion from God to the believers, continually supplying to the believers the riches of God in Christ. This can be considered as the general description of the divine dispensing in 1 and 2 Corinthians. Under this general description, there are five items which speak of the all-inclusive Christ as the power, wisdom, righteousness, sanctification, and redemption from God to the believers.

Christ as the all-inclusive One belongs to all the believers. He is jointly participated in by all of them (1 Cor. 1:2b). He is our portion, given to us by God (Col. 1:12). Furthermore, He is the One into whom God has called the believers. First Corinthians 1:9 says: "God is faithful, through whom you were called into the fellowship of His Son, Jesus Christ our Lord." This shows us we have partaken of the union with

Jesus Christ the Son of God and have jointly participated in His fellowship. God has called us into such a fellowship, to enjoy Christ as God's portion dispensed to us, which includes power, wisdom, righteousness, sanctification, and redemption. These five items contain the divine and rich dispensing of God. God has dispensed Christ as these five items to us.

Who is Christ? Christ is the embodiment of the Triune God. For God to give us Christ is for Him to give us Himself. As what is He being given to us? To say that He is given to us to be our Savior and Redeemer is a shallow understanding. To say that He is given to us as life goes a little deeper. From 1 Corinthians 1 we see that God has given us Christ, that is, He has given us Himself, to be our power, wisdom, righteousness, sanctification, and redemption. Every one of these five items is simply Christ Himself. Christ is the power, wisdom, righteousness, sanctification, and redemption given by God to us. This is true not only on the day of regeneration, but thereafter Christ is continually given by God to us. This is like the electricity in the power station. From the day the house was built and the power lines installed, electricity has been transmitted continually into the house and has been made available for the operation of every electric appliance.

From the time we first called, "O Lord Jesus, I believe in You; I receive You," the Lord Jesus as the heavenly electricity has been connected to us, and the transmission has begun. From that day on, it has never stopped. As far as I am concerned, during the past sixty-five years, there has continually been a transmission from God to me. With every one of us who is a regenerated and saved person, there is such a transmission within. Although at times we are weak, in darkness, and even sin and are temporarily cut off, we are forgiven and are connected once again whenever we turn and confess our sins. The transmission of Christ resumes, and we can enjoy Christ as our power, wisdom, righteousness, sanctification, and redemption.

BEING THE DIVINE DISPENSING AS THE POWER FROM GOD TO THE BELIEVERS

First Corinthians 1:24 tells us that the crucified Christ

is the power of God. Christ as the power of God is with a dynamic power; He strengthens the believers, supplying and sustaining them in what they are and what they do. In all our circumstances and conditions, Christ as the power from God first enables us to suffer, second, enables us to bear the burdens, third, sustains us unshakable, and fourth, enables us to stand firm. This can be compared to what Paul said, "I can do all things in Him who empowers me" (Phil. 4:13). Christ as the power of God is daily supplying and sustaining us through His divine dispensing.

BEING THE DIVINE DISPENSING AS THE WISDOM FROM GOD TO THE BELIEVERS

First Corinthians 1:24 also tells us that the crucified Christ is the wisdom of God. Through Christ's incarnation and crucifixion, God removed man's sins and annulled Satan, the one who corrupted man, thus releasing the divine life and making it available to all those who believe in Him. This is God's wisdom. This wisdom is full of counsel, affording the saints the strategies. In the church life today, as long as we have Christ as our wisdom from God, all the problems will no longer continue to be problems.

BEING THE DIVINE DISPENSING AS THE RIGHTEOUSNESS FROM GOD TO THE BELIEVERS

Christ as the righteousness from God to us (1 Cor. 1:30) is not only for justification concerning our past offenses, but is for our living today. It enables us to be right and just toward God, man, and everything else in procedures and methods. Christ is dispensed from God into us to be our life, power, and wisdom, so that we can live out this righteous living and be righteous in every word, deed, movement, and action.

BEING THE DIVINE DISPENSING AS THE SANCTIFICATION FROM GOD TO THE BELIEVERS

Christ as the sanctification from God to us (1 Cor. 1:30) is not only sanctifying us in position, but in disposition also, so that we can be set apart to God from everything common. He is the power of our sanctification, and He is also the factor for our sanctification. Through Him, the divine dispensing is continually transmitted into us, sanctifying our whole being—spirit, soul, and body—making us holy, full of the divine element to live out an excelling living.

BEING THE DIVINE DISPENSING AS THE REDEMPTION FROM GOD TO THE BELIEVERS

Finally, Christ as the redemption from God to us (1 Cor. 1:30) will transfigure our body through His divine life, so that we will have the body of His glory (Phil. 3:21). Here we need to realize that everything that God glorifies has to be redeemed by passing through the judgment of the cross. First, there is redemption, then glory. More or less, every one of us is still in the old creation and in the natural life. For this reason, we need to take the judgment of the cross in order that we can receive Christ as our redemption and can be qualified to enjoy God's glory. This is not only for the believers' living today, but for the redemption of their bodies in the future, so that their whole being can enter into God's glory and can express God's glory and radiance forever.

Today, in the church life, every day we need the all-inclusive Christ to be our power, wisdom, righteousness, sanctification, and redemption. All the divine riches of Christ are being continually dispensed from God into us. The more He is dispensed into us, the more the divine element within us increases, so that eventually our whole being is supplied and sustained by Him.

(A message given by Brother Witness Lee in Kuching, Malaysia on October 31, 1990)

CHAPTER NINE

THE DIVINE DISPENSING
OF THE ALL-INCLUSIVE CHRIST
IN FEEDING, WATERING, AND TRANSFORMING
THE BELIEVERS

OUTLINE AND SCRIPTURE READING

I. **The all-inclusive Christ being the divine dispensing as the Passover Lamb and the unleavened bread, feeding the believers and supplying them life—1 Cor. 5:7-8:**

1 Corinthians 5:7-8
Purge out the old leaven, that you may be a new lump, even as you are unleavened. For indeed our Passover, Christ, has been sacrificed. (8) Let us therefore keep the feast, not with old leaven, nor with leaven of malice and evil, but with unleavened bread of sincerity and truth.

A. **Not only supplying the believers with the power of life for them to run the God-ordained race of following Him;**

B. **But also supplying the believers with nourishment of life and increasing God's element of growth within them.**

II. **The all-inclusive Christ being the divine dispensing as the spiritual rock out of which flows living water, and as the spiritual bread from heaven, nurturing them and supplying them with life—1 Cor. 10:3-4; John 6:57b-58a:**

1 Corinthians 10:3-4
And all ate the same spiritual food, (4) and all drank the same spiritual drink; for they drank of a

spiritual rock which followed them, and the rock was Christ.

John 6:57b-58a
...he who eats Me shall also live because of Me. (58a) This is the bread which came down out of heaven...

   A. Not only supplying the believers with the life-power for them to run God's race;

   B. But also supplying the believers with the divine element for the growth of God.

III. The all-inclusive Christ being the divine dispensing as the anointing of the compound Spirit, and as the sealing of the seal, saturating and transforming the believers—2 Cor. 1:21-22:

2 Corinthians 1:21-22
But He who firmly attaches us with you unto Christ and has anointed us is God, (22) who has also sealed us and given the pledge of the Spirit in our hearts.

   A. Not only anointing and sealing God's divine element into the entire being of the believers inwardly and outwardly;

   B. But also transforming the believers' nature metabolically by God's divine element that they may have a divine transformation in their entire being.

IV. The all-inclusive Christ being the divine dispensing within the believers as the inscribing of the ink, who is the life-giving Spirit, and outside the believers as the "xeroxing" of the Spirit who transforms them (as a mirror), constituting the believers ministers of the New Testament; these believers reflect His glorious image to fulfill the New Testament ministry—2 Cor. 3:3, 18:

2 Corinthians 3:3
Being manifested that you are a letter of Christ

ministered by us, inscribed not with ink, but with the Spirit of the living God; not in tablets of stone, but in fleshy tablets of the heart.

2 Corinthians 3:18
And we all with unveiled face, beholding and reflecting as a mirror the glory of the Lord, are being transformed into the same image from glory to glory, even as from the Lord Spirit.

A. Not only making the believers the constitution of Christ's life within;

B. But making them Christ's glorious expression without.

In the last message, we saw that Christ is the eternal portion given to us from God. This eternal portion is not a thing, but a living person. He is the embodiment of the Triune God. God in the Son is embodied in a man of flesh and blood. Outwardly speaking, He was a man; but inwardly speaking, He was God. He was a wonderful God-man who was born in a manger, grew up in Nazareth, was crucified on the cross, died and resurrected, and in resurrection became a life-giving Spirit (1 Cor. 15:45b). This is the One whom God has given us to be our common portion (1 Cor. 1:2). He is the One into whom we are called (1 Cor. 1:9). During these few meetings, we have saints coming together from all directions. We may not have known each other before, yet we can pray, praise, and speak in the same way because the factor of our fellowship is Christ Himself.

First Corinthians 1 begins by showing us explicitly and clearly that God has given us Christ as our eternal portion, to be our power, wisdom, righteousness, sanctification, and redemption. God gave His Son to us as our eternal portion, so that we can be supplied and sustained and can live a life that no one can live, endure sufferings that no one can endure, taking ways that no one can take, and doing a work that no one can do. In this way, we become men among men, and men of men. Today, in following the Lord, in serving Him, in administrating the church, and in testifying for the Lord, the best way is to be crucified with the Lord and to live with Him in resurrection. In the church or in His work, whenever we encounter difficulties, criticisms, or even opposition, and it appears that we have come to a dead end, our way out is Christ and His cross. Our whole Christian living, our administration of the church, and the Lord's leading in our service, all depend on our dying and living with Christ. This is the power, and this is the wisdom.

Moreover, Christ has also become our righteousness from God. He is the living righteousness within us, enabling us to live a righteous and proper living. What we live out should not be our own righteousness, good works, or moral behavior, but the righteous Christ. Furthermore, Christ becomes our sanctification from God. He is the power and factor of our sanctification, sanctifying us not only positionally, but dispositionally, so that our whole being, spirit, soul, and body, will be fully sanctified. In the end, Christ becomes our redemption from God. Everything in us that is of the natural being, the flesh, self, the world, sin, the old creation, and everything satanic has to be crucified on the cross and judged by God before we can be redeemed and glorified. Superficially speaking, the book of 1 Corinthians deals with all the confusion, division, and improper situations in the church in Corinth. Actually, it reveals to us the all-inclusive Christ, the One who has died and resurrected, and His cross. Hence, in order to solve the problems in the church, we have to give Christ the proper ground in us and among us, so that He can be our everything, and we can receive His dispensing. In this way, whatever problem we have, whether it is a relationship among the saints, between husbands and wives, or with unbelievers, will be solved readily when we experience the death of Christ and live in His resurrection.

This is the picture shown in 1 Corinthians 1. It depicts a group of people satisfying the desire of God's heart and produced according to His economy through His dispensing and Christ's redemption in death and resurrection. All of us should be this kind of people, having Christ as our power, wisdom, righteousness, sanctification, and redemption within, and being supplied by Him unceasingly. When we all reach this condition, our coming together will be the church, the Body of Christ, as God's habitation, for the expression of God's glory.

THE ALL-INCLUSIVE CHRIST
BEING THE DIVINE DISPENSING AS
THE PASSOVER LAMB AND THE UNLEAVENED BREAD

From 1 Corinthians 2 to the last chapter of 2 Corinthians, there are twenty-eight chapters. They show us the way Christ is worked into the believers through the divine dispensing. From these chapters I have summarized four pairs of items, with eight things. The first pair is described in 1 Corinthians 5:7-8. Christ is the Passover Lamb and the unleavened bread.

Both items are food and are life supplies. The real gospel is not only a matter of the redemption by the blood of the Lamb, but a matter of the life supply of the unleavened bread. On the night the Israelites left Egypt, every house had to kill a lamb and to strike the blood on the two side posts and on the upper doorpost of the house to escape God's judgment. In addition, they had to eat the flesh of the lamb with the unleavened bread and the bitter herbs. While they ate, they had to gird their loins, with shoes on their feet, with their staff in their hand, and they had to eat in haste (Exo. 12:1-11). This was for their supply in life and for their warfare and move. Christ is the Passover Lamb and the unleavened bread; both are for the divine dispensing. Hence, the all-inclusive Christ as the Passover Lamb and as the unleavened bread not only supplies the believers with the power of life to run the God-ordained course of following Him, but supplies the believers with the nourishment of life to increase God's element of growth in them.

This shows us that God's salvation is to dispense Himself to us as our Savior and Redeemer. The way to have this dispensing is to take Christ in as food. Every time we come to the Lord's table to remember Him, we do not come for a religious worship, but to eat and drink of Him. In this way, He will have the true remembrance from us (Matt. 26:26-28; Luke 22:19).

THE ALL-INCLUSIVE CHRIST
BEING THE DIVINE DISPENSING AS
THE SPIRITUAL ROCK OUT OF WHICH FLOWS
THE LIVING WATER AND AS THE SPIRITUAL FOOD
THAT COMES DOWN FROM HEAVEN

The second pair is described in 1 Corinthians 10:3-4, where Christ is the spiritual rock, out of whom flows the living water, and also the spiritual food that comes down from heaven. Christ is the spiritual rock that follows us. Out of Him flows the living water, quenching our thirst and satisfying us. In addition, He is the daily spiritual food that comes down from heaven, becoming our life supply for our journeying. When we eat, drink, and enjoy Him every day, spontaneously, we will live by Him (John 6:57-58). In John 6:63 the Lord Jesus says: "It is the Spirit who gives life; the flesh profits nothing; the words which I have spoken unto you are spirit and are life." The Lord is not giving the flesh of His physical body to us to eat. That flesh, the human flesh, profits nothing. What He gives to man is the life-giving Spirit, who is simply Himself in resurrection.

The whole Bible is full of this kind of thought, which is that God wants us to eat and to receive Him. Now in resurrection, He is the life-giving Spirit. This Spirit is embodied in His word. When we receive His word by exercising our spirit, we are eating and drinking the Lord. By this, we receive the Spirit who is life. Through this, Christ supplies us not only with the life-power for us to run God's race, but with the divine element for God to grow.

THE ALL-INCLUSIVE CHRIST
BEING THE DIVINE DISPENSING AS
THE ANOINTING OF THE COMPOUND SPIRIT
AND AS THE SEALING OF THE SEAL

The third pair is described in 2 Corinthians 1:21-22, where Christ as the compound Spirit is the anointing and the sealing. The holy ointment in Exodus 30 is a type of the compound Spirit of Christ. It is formed by one kind of oil mingled with four kinds of spices, typifying the fact that the Spirit of Christ is a compound Spirit. It includes divinity, humanity, death, the effectiveness of death, resurrection, the fragrance of resurrection, and other elements. When God joins us to Christ the Anointed One, we are anointed by God with Him; that is, we are anointed by the compound Spirit of Christ. This anointing is a dispensing, adding God's divine elements into us. Furthermore, this anointing of the compound Spirit of Christ in us is a sealing, making the divine elements a seal in us, thus expressing the image of God.

Both the anointing and the sealing are a divine dispensing. This dispensing not only waters and saturates us, anointing and sealing us within and without with God's divine element, but it transforms us in our nature metabolically with God's divine element, so that our whole being has a divine transformation.

THE ALL-INCLUSIVE CHRIST
BEING THE DIVINE DISPENSING AS
THE INSCRIBING OF THE INK, WHO IS
THE LIFE-GIVING SPIRIT, AND AS THE "XEROXING"
OF THE TRANSFORMING SPIRIT

Finally, the fourth pair is found in 2 Corinthians 3:3 and 18. Here we have the inward inscribing by Christ into the believers with the life-giving Spirit as the ink and the outward "xeroxing" by Christ onto the believers as mirrors with His transforming Spirit. As those enjoying Christ, we are the letters of Christ, where the Spirit of the living God, as the living God Himself, and as the element of the inscribing ink, supplies us with Christ as the content, with the result that He is expressed in us, and He is known and read by all men. This is the inward aspect. But there is also the outward aspect, which is that we, the believers, are like a mirror. With unveiled face, we behold Christ. Christ is reflected on our face, and we are gradually transformed into the image of Christ.

Through this twofold divine dispensing, Christ will constitute us the ministers of the New Testament, and we will reflect His glorious image, thus fulfilling the New Testament ministry. As a result, not only will we become the very constitution of the life of Christ within, but we will become the glorious expression of Christ without.

This is God's eternal economy, which is accomplished through the many-fold dispensing of the all-inclusive Christ. In conclusion, after the Triune God has been processed through death and resurrection to become the Spirit and has entered into us, He begins His dispensing. He dispenses the all-inclusive Christ to us as power, wisdom, righteousness, sanctification, and redemption. In addition, He also dispenses Christ to us as the Passover Lamb and the unleavened bread, as the spiritual rock out of which flows the living water, as the spiritual food from heaven, as the anointing and the sealing, as the inscribing of the inward ink, and as the xeroxing in the outward reflection. By this, we receive such a Christ for our supply, sustenance, feeding, watering, and transformation.

(A message given by Brother Witness Lee in Kuching, Malaysia on November 1, 1990)

CHAPTER TEN

THE DIVINE DISPENSING
OF THE ALL-INCLUSIVE CHRIST
BECOMING THE FACTOR FOR THE GROWTH
AND THE BUILDING UP OF THE CHURCH

OUTLINE AND SCRIPTURE READING

I. **The all-inclusive Christ being the divine dispensing as the foundation for the building up of the church, uplifting and supplying the believers with the nourishing element for their growth in life—1 Cor. 3:11, 6-7:**

1 Corinthians 3:11
For other foundation no one is able to lay besides that which is being laid, which is Jesus Christ.

1 Corinthians 3:6-7
I planted, Apollos watered, but God made to grow; (7) so that neither is the one who plants anything nor the one who waters, but the One who makes to grow, God.

A. **Not only as the foundation for saints to be built up—1 Cor. 3:12a;**

1 Corinthians 3:12a
But if anyone builds on the foundation...

B. **But also becoming the divine dispensing which transforms the believers in the divine life into the precious materials for the building up of the church—1 Cor. 3:12b.**

1 Corinthians 3:12b
...gold, silver, precious stones...

II. **The all-inclusive Christ equipping the believers with the divine dispensing of the Spirit who dispenses the spiritual gifts to the believers, supplying them with the spiritual capacity, for the building up of the Body of Christ—1 Cor. 12:4, 7-11:**

1 Corinthians 12:4
But there are distributions of gifts, but the same Spirit.

1 Corinthians 12:7-11
But to each one is given the manifestation of the Spirit for profit. (8) For to one through the Spirit is given a word of wisdom, and to another a word of knowledge, according to the same Spirit; (9) to a different one faith in the same Spirit, and to another gifts of healing in the one Spirit; (10) and to another operations of works of power, and to another prophecy, and to another discerning of spirits; to a different one various kinds of tongues, and to another interpretation of tongues. (11) But the one and the same Spirit operates all these things, distributing to each one individually as He purposes.

A. **Not only having a part in the Lord's ministry in the building up of His Body through the gifts and functions of the dispensing Spirit— 1 Cor. 12:5;**

1 Corinthians 12:5
And there are distributions of ministries, and the same Lord.

B. **But also having a part in the operation by which God accomplishes His eternal economy through the same gifts and functions— 1 Cor. 12:6.**

1 Corinthians 12:6
And there are distributions of operations, but the same God, who is operating all things in all.

III. **The divine dispensing of the all-inclusive Christ in the beholding of His glory by the believers who seek after Him and serve Him, enabling them to receive His divine element and be transformed into His image from glory to glory— 2 Cor. 3:18:**

2 Corinthians 3:18
And we all with unveiled face, beholding and reflecting as a mirror the glory of the Lord, are being transformed into the same image from glory to glory, even as from the Lord Spirit.

A. **Constituting them ministers of the New Testament for the building up of the Body of Christ—2 Cor. 3:6.**

2 Corinthians 3:6
Who also made us sufficient as ministers of a new covenant, not of letter, but of the Spirit; for the letter kills, but the Spirit gives life.

B. **Enabling them to bear the New Testament ministry which bears Christ's glorious image and which dispenses Him—2 Cor. 4:1.**

2 Corinthians 4:1
Therefore, having this ministry, as we received mercy we do not lose heart.

IV. **The all-inclusive Christ being the divine dispensing as the treasure within the believers in their serving and preaching of Him—2 Cor. 4:7a:**

2 Corinthians 4:7a
But we have this treasure in earthen vessels...

A. **Constituting them ministers of the New Testament—2 Cor. 3:6.**

2 Corinthians 3:6
Who also made us sufficient as ministers of a new covenant, not of letter, but of the Spirit; for the letter kills, but the Spirit gives life.

B. **Enabling them with the excelling power to fulfill their New Testament ministry of the preaching of the gospel for the building up of the church—2 Cor. 4:7b, 2-4.**

2 Corinthians 4:7b
...that the excellence of the power may be of God and not of us.

2 Corinthians 4:2-4
But we have renounced the hidden things of shame, not walking in craftiness nor adulterating the word of God, but by the manifestation of the truth commending ourselves to every man's conscience before God. (3) And if also our gospel is veiled, it is veiled in those who are perishing, (4) in whom the god of this age has blinded the thoughts of the unbelieving, so that the illumination of the gospel of the glory of Christ, who is the image of God, should not shine in them.

V. **The all-inclusive Christ being the divine dispensing as God's sufficient grace to be Christ's power—2 Cor. 12:9:**

2 Corinthians 12:9
And He has said to me, My grace is sufficient for you, for My power is perfected in weakness. Most gladly therefore will I rather boast in my weaknesses, that the power of Christ might tabernacle over me.

A. **Not only as the believers' power for laboring more abundantly for God—1 Cor. 15:10;**

1 Corinthians 15:10
But by the grace of God I am what I am; and His grace unto me was not in vain, but I labored more abundantly than all of them, yet not I, but the grace of God with me.

B. **But also becoming the rich enjoyment and**

harvest of the believers in their labor for God—1 Cor. 15:58.

1 Corinthians 15:58
Wherefore, my beloved brothers, be steadfast, immovable, always abounding in the work of the Lord, knowing that your labor is not in vain in the Lord.

From the past messages, we have received a vision. Our God has a divine economy, which is to dispense Himself in Christ to His chosen ones, those who believe in Him. From the time we were saved and regenerated, the Christ who is the embodiment of God has been dispensed into us to be our life, our supply, and everything to us, so that we are righteous, we are sanctified, and we are redeemed. This is not human ethics, philosophy, or religion. Rather, it is the Triune God processed and dispensed into us, and then living out from us. Now we are children of God and members of Christ. Daily we receive the transfusion from Christ, and moment by moment we receive the nourishment of life. As a result, we grow in the life of God, and we are coordinated and built up together to be a corporate vessel, which is the church, the Body of Christ, and the habitation of God. This is the goal of God's economy.

For this reason, after we are regenerated, we have to learn not to live by ourselves but to live by Christ, daily living a life of death and resurrection. In this way God's element can be added into us day by day, and we can be gradually delivered from the natural self. When we live Christ this way, the church will be manifested.

Now we will pick out some important verses from 1 and 2 Corinthians to prove that Christ becomes our life within and our living without for the purpose of building up His church.

THE ALL-INCLUSIVE CHRIST
BEING THE DIVINE DISPENSING
AS THE FOUNDATION FOR
THE BUILDING UP OF THE CHURCH

First Corinthians 3:11 says: "For other foundation no one is able to lay besides that which is being laid, which is Jesus Christ." Christ is God's unique foundation for the building up of the church. He is a living foundation stone that supports the church. At the same time that He is supporting the church, He is also supplying the church (1 Cor. 3:6-7). He supplies the need of our life within, so that we grow by Him. Through this, we are also being supported together.

From 1 Corinthians 3 we can see the growth and the building up of the church. On one hand, the church is God's farm. This farm will produce plant life when there is planting, watering, and growth. On the other hand, the church is God's building, with precious minerals such as the gold, the silver, and the precious stones as proper materials for the building. From the growth of the plants to the building up of the minerals, there is a transformation process. Hence, Christ is not only the foundation for the believers to be built up (1 Cor. 3:12a); He is also the divine dispensing by which the believers are transformed in the divine life into the precious materials of the church (1 Cor. 3:12b). The more we receive Christ's dispensing and grow in God's life, the more our inward nature will be transformed by God's element to become the material for the building up of the church.

EQUIPPING THE BELIEVERS
WITH THE DIVINE DISPENSING
OF THE SPIRIT
WHO DISTRIBUTES SPIRITUAL GIFTS

First Corinthians 12:4 says: "But there are distributions of gifts, but the same Spirit." From this we can see that the spiritual gifts are distributed by the Spirit. This is why we have to learn to live in the spirit and not in ourselves, so that the Spirit will have the ground to spread within us. This spreading Spirit will become our gift. For this reason, when you come to the meeting, I would strongly exhort all of you to first learn to pray. This is the simplest thing to do. Second, you have to learn to testify. Third, you have to learn to prophesy for the Lord. If you would practice this way and would seize the opportunity to pray, testify, or prophesy in the meeting, the gift of the Holy Spirit will be able to spread within you, and spontaneously your function will be realized.

For many years, among us we have spoken about the church services, and we have encouraged the saints to participate in them. But the church services that we talked about were mostly business affairs, such as cleaning, hall arranging, ushering, and hospitality. These things do have their place. But the real service of the church lies not so much in the business affairs as in the spiritual matters. While you are taking care of this special conference, it is right for you to do your best to meet the needs in the business affairs. But when you come to the meetings, you should release your spirit, and you should pray in a strong way, one after another. Your testimonies should be to the point, and your prophesying should be with much content. If you practice this way again and again, exercising your spirit, your mind, your utterance, and your boldness, the meetings will be rich. Only then will the whole church be able to enter the spiritual service. The main thing with the spiritual service is the preaching of the gospel to save sinners, the feeding of the lambs, the mutual shepherding and perfecting, and the prophesying for the Lord. When all the saints have been equipped by the spiritual gifts distributed by the Spirit, the gospel will spread more prevailingly, and more saints will be nourished, cared for, and perfected, and the meetings will become more living and rich.

First Corinthians 12 shows us that Christ is the Head of His Body, equipping and supplying every one of His members with the Spirit who distributes the spiritual gifts, that they would not only be able to participate, by the gift and capacity of the distributing Spirit, in the Lord's ministry of the building up of the Body of Christ (1 Cor. 12:5), but by the same gift and function, would also be able to participate in the operation which is for the accomplishment of His eternal economy (1 Cor. 12:6), unto the building up of the Body of Christ. For this reason, we have to continually receive the dispensing of the Spirit within us and to go along with the operation of the Spirit, so that the gift of the Spirit can spread within us. By this, the spiritual function will be realized, and we will have a part in the ministry of the building up of the church.

Thus, we can see that today, it is not a matter of our waiting for God or for the Spirit; rather, it is Christ, the Spirit, who distributes the spiritual gifts, who is waiting for us. Hence, in the meetings, or outside the meetings, we have to move with the Spirit when He flows within us. By this way, not only will all of us be able to serve in the meetings, but we will be full of spiritual service outside the meetings.

THE ALL-INCLUSIVE CHRIST BEING THE DIVINE DISPENSING IN THE BEHOLDING OF HIS GLORY BY THE BELIEVERS WHO SERVE HIM AND PURSUE AFTER HIM

Second Corinthians 3:18 says: "And we all with unveiled face, beholding and reflecting as a mirror the glory of the Lord, are being transformed into the same image from glory to glory, even as from the Lord Spirit." When we behold the glory of the Lord with unveiled face, the Lord will also unveil Himself and will transfuse us with what He is. We all have this kind of experience. Particularly in the morning, when we open ourselves to the Lord and fellowship with Him face to face, the riches of the Lord will be dispensed into us, and we will be transformed gradually into His glorious image. In this way, we will be constituted the ministers of the New Testament for the building up of the Body of Christ (2 Cor. 3:6). We will be able to help others to salvation and help them to grow and be perfected. We will also be able to have the New Testament ministry which bears the glorious image of Christ and which dispenses Christ (2 Cor. 4:1).

As we are being gradually constituted to be the ministers of the New Testament, we will be able to take up the New Testament ministry. Only then will we be able to bring our acquaintances to believe in the Lord and to be saved. Only then will we be able to nourish the newly saved believers and to teach and perfect the saints one by one. In this way, we will become a person with the New Testament ministry. Among us, if more are like this, the condition of the church will be greatly changed. Not only should we have some spiritual service in the meetings, but we should have spiritual service anywhere and everywhere in our daily life outside the meetings. For us to have a job is simply to make a living. Our real profession is to serve the Lord. The opportunity to serve in the meetings is limited. But in the daily life, there are many opportunities for us to dispense Christ to others.

THE ALL-INCLUSIVE CHRIST
BEING THE DIVINE DISPENSING
AS THE TREASURE WITHIN THE BELIEVERS
WHO SERVE AND PREACH HIM

Second Corinthians 4:7 says: "But we have this treasure in earthen vessels, that the excellence of the power may be of God and not of us." The treasure here is the glorious Christ who is the embodiment of God becoming our life and everything to us. He is living within us, the believers, and He is full of operations. He supplies us continually with the excelling power through His dispensing, constituting us, the worthless and weak vessels, as ministers of the New Testament (2 Cor. 3:6), so that we can fulfill our New Testament ministry, which is the preaching of the gospel for the building up of the church (2 Cor. 4:7b, 2-4).

THE ALL-INCLUSIVE CHRIST
BEING THE DIVINE DISPENSING
AS GOD'S SUFFICIENT GRACE

Second Corinthians 12:9a says: "And He has said to me, My grace is sufficient for you, for My power is perfected in weakness." The grace here is Christ Himself who has passed through death and resurrection, dispensed into us in resurrection and becoming our supply and enjoyment. It is by this grace that Paul labored more than the other apostles. He labored much for God, yet he said that it was not him, but the grace of God being with him (1 Cor. 15:10). Hence, for the living and service of the church, we need to daily contact and fellowship with Christ as God's grace, so that His riches can be continually dispensed into us as the grace we enjoy. In this way, we will have the power of Christ tabernacling over us; we will be able to labor more for God and to do what the Lord wants us to do. In the end, the all-inclusive Christ will become our rich enjoyment in our labor for God, and we will reap an abounding harvest (1 Cor. 15:58), which is the perfecting of the saints and the building up of the church.

(A message given by Brother Witness Lee in Kuching, Malaysia on November 2, 1990)

SECTION IV

The Divine Dispensing of the Divine Trinity and the Producing and Building Up of the Church

CHAPTER ELEVEN

THE DIVINE DISPENSING
OF THE DIVINE TRINITY PRODUCING
THE CHURCH AS THE BODY OF CHRIST

OUTLINE AND SCRIPTURE READING

I. **The divine dispensing of God the Father:**

A. **In choosing the believers in Christ, that His chosen believers may have His divine nature and thus may be sanctified—Eph. 1:4.**

Ephesians 1:4
According as He chose us in Him before the foundation of the world that we should be holy and without blemish before Him, in love.

B. **In predestinating the believers through Christ, that His predestinated believers may have His divine life and thus may become His sons—Eph. 1:5.**

Ephesians 1:5
Having predestinated us unto sonship through Jesus Christ to Himself, according to the good pleasure of His will.

II. **The divine dispensing of God the Son in redeeming the believers, that His redeemed believers:**

A. **May be put in Christ.**

B. **May have Christ as their element and sphere, and thus may be made God's inheritance according to God's economy by such a dispensing of His divine element—Eph. 1:7, 10-11.**

Ephesians 1:7
In whom we have redemption through His

blood, the forgiveness of offenses, according to the riches of His grace.

Ephesians 1:10-11
Unto a dispensation of the fullness of the times, to head up all things in Christ, the things in the heavens and the things on the earth, in Him, (11) in whom also we were made an inheritance, having been predestinated according to the purpose of the One who operates all things according to the counsel of His will.

III. **The divine dispensing of God the Spirit as the sealing and pledging in the believers, that the believers:**

A. **May be sealed unto God's image, as a mark that they are God's inheritance—Eph. 1:13.**

Ephesians 1:13
In whom you also, hearing the word of the truth, the gospel of your salvation, in whom also believing, you were sealed with the Holy Spirit of the promise.

B. **May have a foretaste of God as the blessing of the believers' inheritance—Eph. 1:14.**

Ephesians 1:14
Who is the pledge of our inheritance, unto the redemption of the acquired possession to the praise of His glory.

IV. **The divine dispensing of the Triune God in the transmission to the believers by the surpassingly great power that He wrought in Christ, with the threefold divine dispensing of God the Father, God the Son, and God the Spirit, producing the church:**

A. **As the Body of Christ.**

B. **As the fullness of the One who fills all in all—Eph. 1:19-23.**

Ephesians 1:19-23
And what is the surpassing greatness of His power toward us who believe, according to the operation of the might of His strength, (20) which He wrought in Christ in raising Him from among the dead, and seating Him at His right hand in the heavenlies, (21) far above all rule and authority and power and lordship, and every name that is named, not only in this age, but also in that which is coming; (22) and He subjected all things under His feet, and gave Him to be Head over all things to the church, (23) which is His Body, the fullness of the One who fills all in all.

This series of messages that we are releasing this time will emphasize the divine dispensing of the Divine Trinity. From this message on, we will consider the divine dispensing of the Divine Trinity from the book of Ephesians. I hope that we would all pray much so that the Lord would allow us not only to hear them, but to see them. Superficially, the words in the Bible say one thing, but when we dive into them and experience them, it is another thing. This is especially true with a book as deep as Ephesians. On the surface, the book is not too difficult to understand, but when one probes into it, he will realize that it is not too easy. Ephesians 1:4-5 says that God has chosen us before the foundation of the world that we should become holy before Him, and that He has also predestinated us unto sonship through Jesus Christ. Superficially speaking, the expressions "to be holy" and "to have the sonship" are not too difficult to understand. But if anyone asks how we, the common people, can become holy, and how we, the sons of men who are born of men, can receive God's sonship, it will be very difficult to explain. If we try to find out further how in experience we can become holy and receive God's sonship, we will find it even more difficult to understand. We can say that on the surface, the entire book of Ephesians does not mention the term the divine dispensing. Actually, every point concerns the divine dispensing.

GOD NOT WANTING MAN TO WORK BY HIMSELF

Before we come to this message, I would first fellowship one thing with all of you. God's economy, that is, His plan, purpose, and arrangement of things to accomplish His desire, is carried out in ways very different from ours. For example, God wants us to please Him. When we read this word, immediately we would make up our mind, pray, and even fast, saying, "God, be gracious to me. I do have the desire to please You. But You know that I have all kinds of obstacles, problems, and weaknesses. I cannot do it. Please help me." Everyone would justify this kind of prayer and would think that it is right. But although God wants us to please Him, He has no intention that we please Him by our own effort. Rather, He wants us to please Him through living by His life, and even by Himself. Verse 1 of *Hymns*, #499 says: "Oh, what a life! Oh, what a peace! The Christ who's all within me lives." This is the overall subject of the hymn. However, in the experience of many people, for Christ to live within is not peaceful, but bothersome. The above hymn continues to say: "With Him I have been crucified; This glorious fact to me He gives." What is this glorious fact? "Now it's no longer I that live, But Christ the Lord within me lives." It is no longer I that live. This is truly wonderful! Now it is Christ that lives. This is glorious! However, is it really true that from morning until evening, it is no longer I that live, but Christ within me lives? Even today, from morning to evening, is it no longer I that live? I know that most of us would say that sometimes it is He and not we. But most of the time it is we and not He. This is our real condition.

We have to realize one thing here. From Genesis to Revelation the Bible tells us that God requires man to do many things. But He has no intention that man would do them by himself. God wants man to do these things, but He has no intention for man to do them by himself. Everything that God wants us to do is something that we cannot do in ourselves. God says that we have to honor our parents, but we cannot do it. God says that we have to be humble, but we cannot be humble. It is true that God wants everyone of us to be humble. But He has no intention that we be humble by ourselves. Rather, God wants us to be humble by depending on Him. This is why the New Testament has the expression "in Christ" or "in the Lord." We have to walk in love in the Lord. It is God's commandment to us that we walk in love. But He has no intention that we walk in love by ourselves, because we have no love in ourselves. On the contrary, we are full of hatred. If we have no love in ourselves, how can we live by our love? Hence, we have to remember well that God has chosen us to be holy. But He does not need us to accomplish this work of being made holy. We cannot accomplish it or fulfill it. It is also true that God has predestinated us unto sonship. But He has no intention that we obtain the sonship by ourselves either.

GOD'S WAY BEING ACCOMPLISHED
BY DISPENSING

God's way is to do everything Himself and work His holiness into us. This is dispensing. He wants us to be holy, but He has no intention for us to take upon ourselves the work of holiness. Rather, He is working His holy and divine element, that is, His nature, into us to be our element. This results in our becoming holy. God is adding His divine nature into us. This is what we mean by dispensing. God wants us to have the sonship. But we cannot achieve this. Now God is giving His Son to us. Paul testified that at one time he was very zealous for God. But one day God showed him that His pleasure was to reveal His Son in him (Gal. 1:15, 16). For God to reveal His Son in Paul was for Him to dispense His Son into Paul. By this, Paul became a son of God with the sonship, that is, the life, the position, and the nature of the Son of God. As such, he could live the life of a son and enjoy the sonship. This is what we mean by dispensing. Tonight, we want to consider this matter specifically from Ephesians chapter one.

THE DIVINE DISPENSING
OF THE DIVINE TRINITY

The dispensing spoken of in Ephesians is the dispensing of the Divine Trinity. Our God is one, yet He is triune. He is one God, yet He is the Father, the Son, and the Spirit. This is a fact. Our God is unique and only One. Yet He is three, the Father, the Son, and the Spirit. He is God the Father, God the Son, and God the Spirit. When He dispenses Himself, He does so through His Divine Trinity.

THE DIVINE DISPENSING
OF GOD THE FATHER

Chapter one of Ephesians begins by showing us the dispensing of God the Father (Eph. 1:4-5). The Father's dispensing is seen in His choosing us in Christ before the foundation of the world. The purpose of His choosing is for us to become holy. Immediately after choosing us, He predestinated us. His purpose in predestinating us is that we would receive the sonship through His Son. Both the choosing and the predestination speak of His dispensing. He chose us to be holy. This indicates that He has given us His divine nature. With His divine nature, we can become holy. Some may say that since the Father's choosing was before the foundation of the world, there was no dispensing yet. However, with God there is no element of time. Thus, in God's eyes, at the very time that He chose us, although we were not yet created, and although the heavens and the earth were not yet made, in His foreknowledge He saw us already, chose us, and gave us His nature in order that we might become holy. This is dispensing.

After God the Father chose us, He marked us out and predestinated us unto sonship. Hence, in order for God to make us holy, He gave us His holy nature, and in order for us to become His sons and have the sonship, He gave us His life. We are not God's adopted sons. Rather, we are the children begotten by God's life. John 1:12 says, "As many as received Him, to them He gave authority to become children of God." These are not born of blood, nor of the will of the flesh, nor of the will of man, but of God. For God to predestinate us unto sonship means that He begets us and dispenses His life into us. Hence, God has not only put His nature into us to make us holy, but has imparted His life into us to make us His sons. Both of these involve God's dispensing.

Since God has chosen us to be holy, we do not need to struggle to be holy by ourselves. What we have to do is realize that God has chosen us and put His nature within us at the time of His choosing. Hence, we do not need to strive or struggle. Instead, we only need to fellowship with our Father. Every morning when we wake up, we should say to the Father, "Abba, Father, You are my Father. You have given me Your life and Your nature. Praise You that I can be Your son and can become holy." If we would do this, I can guarantee you that we would be holy the entire morning. Before lunch we should say a few words like these to our Father again. At every meal we should say something to our Father. This will be a shield to protect us from the distractions and attacks of the evil one, and will make us holy. God has no intention for us to become holy by ourselves. Before the creation of the heavens and the earth, He already put His life and nature within us. As long as we live a life of enjoying our Father every day, we will surely become holy. This is the dispensing of God the Father.

THE DIVINE DISPENSING
OF GOD THE SON TO THE BELIEVERS

God the Son is also dispensing His divine riches into us (Eph. 1:7, 10-11). Based on the choosing and predestinating of God the Father, we have the redemption of God the Son.

Putting the Believers into Christ

Although the Father chose and predestinated us, and gave us His life and nature, we became fallen in Adam. For this reason we need redemption. Without the redemption of the Son, even if the Father wanted to give us His life and nature, He could not do it. This is because on our side there is the problem of sin. Hence, God the Son came to accomplish redemption. He died for us, bore our sins away, and redeemed us. God also forgave us in Christ. Once a person believes in the Lord, he is redeemed and put into Christ (1 Cor. 1:30). Once he is in Christ, his sins are forgiven, death is over, and all of his problems are solved. This is the dispensing of the Son into us. This passage in Ephesians shows us a number of times that when we believe in the Lord, we are put into Christ. This is not superstition or empty terminology. Rather, it is a fact. He is the real One. He is the Spirit, the reality, and the grace. When we are in Him, we are in the reality and in grace. Hence, Christ becomes our sphere and our element. In this sphere we are protected, and in this element we enjoy all the divine benefits.

Having Christ as
the Believers' Element and Sphere,
Being Made God's Inheritance according to
God's Economy by the Divine Dispensing
of His Divine Element

There is a short song following Lesson 25 of the *Life Lessons* which says,

I'm in Christ, now rejoicing—
From old Adam I am free!
All old things are becoming
Both new and heavenly!
Praise God! I'm tasting and enjoying
Life and peace and liberty!
Praise God! I'm in Christ eternally!

If every morning, afternoon, and evening and even before we go to bed, we would sing this song concerning our being in Christ, we will be victorious every day. While we sing, the Spirit will operate in us and bring us into the reality. In this way we will be in Christ, and Christ will become our sphere and element. With this divine element, God will make those who are in Christ His chosen inheritance. We are not only God's redeemed ones in Christ, but His precious inheritance produced in Christ and with Christ as our sphere and element, so that God can inherit us. God has purchased us with the blood of His Son. Now we are in His Son, and His Son has become our sphere and our element. If we live in Christ every day, Christ will become our sphere and element, that is, the producing ingredient with which God will make us His inheritance. This is the dispensing of God the Son.

None of us can redeem ourselves, and none of us can become an encircling sphere and an element to make ourselves a precious inheritance to God. Only Christ Himself, God the Son, can dispense to us such a blessing so that He becomes our sphere to surround and protect us, and also our element for our daily enjoyment, so that day by day we may be made more and more precious and may become God's precious inheritance. This is the dispensing of God the Son.

THE DIVINE DISPENSING OF GOD THE SPIRIT
AS THE SEALING AND PLEDGING IN THE BELIEVERS

After speaking of the Father's choosing and predestinating, and the Son's redeeming through which He has become our sphere and element so that we might be made God's precious inheritance, Ephesians 1 speaks of the dispensing of God the Spirit as the sealing and the pledging in the believers.

Being Sealed unto God's Image, as a Mark of God's Inheritance

God the Spirit put Himself into us as our seal. This seal seals us unto God's image, as a mark of God's inheritance. The "ink" used in this seal never dries; it will remain wet forever. This ink will saturate and permeate our entire being. In the beginning of our Christian life, the image imprinted by the seal is not very clear. But the more the seal seals us, the clearer and more distinct the image becomes. Moreover, the seal expands until our whole being—body, soul, and spirit—is saturated with this seal. In ourselves we could never carry out such a sealing, but God has dispensed His Spirit as a seal into us to seal us. Once this seal is on us, we can never remove it.

Having a Foretaste of God as the Blessing of the Believers' Inheritance

The Spirit within us is not only a seal that permeates and saturates us, but He is also a foretaste within us for our enjoyment.

When I was young, I was taught that when a person was filled with the Holy Spirit, he would have the living water flowing out of him. Because of this word, I sought after this experience by praying and confessing my sins. One day I was brought to a Pentecostal meeting. There I saw some people jumping, some rolling on the floor, and some laughing. I was told that these people were filled with the Holy Spirit. But I could not accept that kind of being "filled with the Holy Spirit." Later, the Lord raised up a church in my home. We did not laugh, jump, or shout; we simply prayed, met, sought after the Lord, and preached the gospel in a quiet way. Not far from us was a Pentecostal meeting. One day the leading one from that group attempted to convince me to accept the Pentecostal practices. I pointed out to him that when the church began to meet in my home, only about ten saints attended the meetings, whereas the number in his meetings might have been a little larger. After a period of time, the number in our meetings increased to over eight hundred, while the number in his meetings, after all their jumping, shouting, and being "filled with the Holy Spirit," still remained only forty or fifty.

I say these things to point out to you through my many years of experience that God has no intention for us to jump and shout; in fact, all the things of life that God has given to us are quiet and calm. We go to bed on time, sleep calmly, rise calmly, wash up, pray-read, take our breakfast, do our work, and study calmly. Other than some physical exercise, we do everything in a calm way. To live this way is most healthy. It is the same with the plant life. In growing flowers, it is harmful to over-fertilize or water too much. We should not disturb the plants too much. Instead, we should allow them to live calmly. Even if we do not water the plants, sometimes the heavens will give them water and make them grow. Sometimes we are "cold" toward the Lord; we may not even go to the meetings anymore. At other times we may love the Lord so much that we become very zealous. Formerly, it was difficult just to read through a half of a chapter in the Bible. Now it is easy to read through five chapters a day. But because both our "coldness" and our "hotness" are something of ourselves, they do not last. Only those who are unhurried and steady will remain and persevere.

Since we have the Spirit in us as a seal, pledge, and fore-taste, every morning when we wake up, we should spend ten to fifteen minutes to open up the Lord's Word and read two or three verses successively. We do not need to shout or yell. Of course, we should call on the Lord. This is like our breathing. But we do not need to seek for a feeling. We should simply pray and pray-read several verses in a calm and ordinary way. We should do this every day, fellowshipping with the Lord all the time. We should refrain from anything that gives us unrest and do the things that make us feel peaceful and make the Lord happy. When there is a meeting, we should always attend. In the meetings, we do not have to be that excited; there is no need to stand up to shout or yell. If we have anything to say, we simply say it in a calm way. If we have any testimony to give, we share it in a quiet way. If we continue to live this kind of steady life, we will surely be a healthy Christian. We will enjoy the Father's continual transfusing and dispensing of the life of His Son and His divine nature into us.

We have to realize that very few spiritual things are accomplished once for all. As with our physical life, most spiritual things must be repeated again and again. For example, we need to eat, drink, and breathe for our physical life every day; we cannot graduate from these things. However, we do not need to do these things excessively; we simply need to do them in small portions over a long period of time. Likewise, the calmer our Christian life is, the better it will be. Daily we should allow the Father to dispense His life and nature into us. This can be compared to electricity, which steadily flows bit by bit into the house. If too much comes in all at once, it will be dangerous. We must see first that whatever our God wants us to do, He does not want us to do it by our own striving, but by Him. Second, whatever God gives to us is not given all at once so that it becomes unbearable to us. Rather, it is given bit by bit. For this reason, we have to live a steady and normal Christian life. The less special and the more normal we are, the better.

THE DIVINE DISPENSING OF THE TRIUNE GOD IN THE TRANSMISSION TO THE BELIEVERS BY THE SURPASSINGLY GREAT POWER THAT HE WROUGHT IN CHRIST, WITH THE DIVINE DISPENSING OF GOD THE FATHER, GOD THE SON, AND GOD THE SPIRIT

The dispensing of God the Father is in His choosing us to be holy and predestinating us to have His sonship. The dispensing of God the Son is in His redeeming us so that we can be saved into Himself to be made God's precious inheritance. The dispensing of God the Spirit is in His sealing us and being our enjoyment and foretaste. In this way, daily we receive the dispensing from God the Father, God the Son, and God the Spirit. As a result, the Father, the Son, and the Spirit as the Divine Trinity becomes our divine dispensing, and we enjoy Him every day.

Finally, Ephesians 1 shows us that God's surpassingly great power operated in Christ to resurrect Him from Hades, the grave, and death. This great power also caused Him to ascend to the heavens, seated Him on the throne, and made Him the Head over all things. All of this was accomplished by the surpassingly great power which God operated in Christ. Although this power operates in Christ, it is toward us. The term "toward us" conveys the sense of transmission. God has raised Christ from among the dead, seated Him at His right hand in the heavenlies, subjected all things under His feet, and made Him the Head over all things. All these accomplishments are "to the church." All that God has accomplished in Christ has been transmitted to the church today. This transmission is a kind of continual dispensing. It can be compared to the transmission of electricity into a building. By such a transmission, the building and all of the electrical systems in the building "enjoy" the dispensing of the electricity.

Producing the Church as the Body of Christ and as the Fullness of the One Who Fills All in All

Christ in us is like electricity. Every day He is transmitting, and this transmission is a dispensing. The result of this transmission, this dispensing, is that the church is produced. This church is the Body of Christ, the fullness of the One who fills all in all. Because Christ is so great, all-inclusive, all-extensive, and fills all in all, He needs a universal Body which is the church. By the dispensing of the Father, the dispensing of the Son, the dispensing of the Spirit, plus the all-surpassing transmission of Christ, God has transmitted Himself into us. The result is the producing of the church. The church is not an organization, nor is it merely a gathering of the believers. When we enjoy the dispensing of the Divine Trinity, and come together to transmit this dispensing to others, making it their enjoyment as well, that is the church.

(A message given by Brother Witness Lee in Petaling Jaya, Malaysia on November 3, 1990)

CHAPTER TWELVE

THE DIVINE DISPENSING
OF THE DIVINE TRINITY CAUSING
THE BELIEVERS TO BECOME
GOD'S MASTERPIECE, THE NEW MAN,
GOD'S KINGDOM FOR HIS ADMINISTRATION,
GOD'S HOUSE FOR THE DISPENSING
OF HIS LOVE, AND GOD'S DWELLING PLACE
FOR HIS REST

OUTLINE AND SCRIPTURE READING

I. The dispensing of God the Father in the life in God the Son enlivening the believers (who were in death) together with Christ, raising them up together with Christ, and seating them together with Christ in the heavenlies, thereby creating the believers as His masterpiece:

A. To be His church.

B. That He might display in the ages which are coming the surpassing riches of His (the Triune God's) grace of life—Eph. 2:1-10.

Ephesians 2:1-10
And you, being dead in your offenses and sins, (2) in which you once walked according to the age of this world, according to the ruler of the authority of the air, of the spirit who now is operating in the sons of disobedience; (3) among whom also we all behaved ourselves once in the lusts of our flesh, doing the desires of the flesh and of the thoughts, and were by nature children of wrath, even as the rest; (4) but God, being rich in mercy because of His

great love with which He loved us, (5) even
when we were dead in offenses, made us alive
together with Christ (by grace you have been
saved), (6) and raised us up together and seated
us together in the heavenlies in Christ Jesus,
(7) that He might display in the ages which are
coming the surpassing riches of His grace in
kindness toward us in Christ Jesus. (8) For by
grace you have been saved through faith; and
this not of yourselves; it is the gift of God: (9)
not of works that no one should boast. (10) For
we are His workmanship, created in Christ
Jesus for good works, which God before prepared that we should walk in them.

II. **The divine dispensing of God the Son creating
the Jewish and Gentile believers into one new
man, through His death on the cross and with
His divine element, for God to accomplish His
divine economy, thereby causing the two groups
of believers:**

A. **To be reconciled in one Body to God.**

B. **To enjoy Christ as the peace between the two
and between them and God—Eph. 2:11-17.**

Ephesians 2:11-17

Wherefore remember that once you, the nations
in the flesh, those who are called uncir-
cumcision by those who are called circumcision
in the flesh made by hand, (12) that you were at
that time apart from Christ, alienated from the
commonwealth of Israel, and strangers from
the covenants of the promise, having no hope
and without God in the world. (13) But now in
Christ Jesus you who once were far off have
become near in the blood of Christ. (14) For He
Himself is our peace, who has made both one,
and has broken down the middle wall of parti-
tion, the enmity, (15) having abolished in His

flesh the law of the commandments in ordinances, that He might create the two in Himself
into one new man, making peace, (16) and
might reconcile both in one Body to God
through the cross, slaying the enmity by it; (17)
and coming, He preached the gospel of peace to
you who were far off, and peace to those who
were near.

III. **The divine dispensing of God the Spirit enabling
both groups that compose the new man to have
access in Him unto God the Father, thereby
causing the Body as the new man to become:**

A. **The kingdom of the Triune God for His
administration.**

B. **The house of God for the dispensing of His
love.**

C. **The dwelling place of God in the believers'
spirit for His rest—Eph. 2:18-22.**

Ephesians 2:18-22
For through Him we both have access in one
Spirit unto the Father. (19) So then you are no
longer strangers and sojourners, but you are
fellow citizens of the saints and members of
the household of God, (20) being built upon the
foundation of the apostles and prophets, Christ
Jesus Himself being the cornerstone, (21) in
whom all the building, being fitted together, is
growing into a holy temple in the Lord, (22) in
whom you also are being built together into a
dwelling place of God in spirit.

In the previous message, we saw in Ephesians 1 the divine dispensing of the Divine Trinity and how it has produced the church. The Father's choosing dispensed the Father's nature into us so that we can become holy, and His predestination dispensed His life into us so that we can become His sons. Following this, the Son came to redeem us. In the Son's redemption, through Christ's element, God constitutes us His precious inheritance. Then God the Spirit seals us and becomes a pledge to us so that, on one hand, He saturates and permeates us, and on the other hand, He becomes our enjoyment as a foretaste of God becoming the blessing of our inheritance. Finally, the surpassingly great power that the Triune God operated in Christ is transmitted into us to produce the church.

THE DISPENSING OF GOD THE FATHER
IN THE LIFE IN GOD THE SON ENLIVENING
THE BELIEVERS (WHO WERE IN DEATH),
RESURRECTING THEM AND SEATING THEM
IN THE HEAVENLIES, THEREBY CREATING
THEM TO BE HIS MASTERPIECE

In Ephesians 2 Paul continues by first showing us that the dispensing of God the Father in the life in God the Son has enlivened the believers (who were dead in sins) together with Christ, has raised them up together with Christ, and has seated them together with Christ in the heavenlies, thereby creating the believers as His masterpiece to be His church, that He might display in the ages to come the surpassing riches of the Triune God's grace of life (Eph. 2:1-10).

First, Paul shows us, those who have become the church, what kind of persons we were and how God worked on us to make us His masterpiece. In verses 1 through 3 he shows us that we who have been created to be the Body of Christ through God's dispensing were formerly not only sinners but dead ones, being dead in our offenses and sins. In the universe we were nothing. However, through God's great mercy He came to us in His grace, which is the divine life of God in His Son. For God to come to us in His grace is for Him to come to us in the divine life of His Son. Through this divine life,

God enlivened us, the dead ones, with Christ. Christ has died for our sins, and on the third day God raised Christ up. He used this enlivening life to do the work of His masterpiece so that we, the dead ones, could become alive.

After we were made alive, we were resurrected with Christ (v. 6). To be made alive is to wake up, and to resurrect is to stand up and be able to move around. Moreover, in resurrection God has raised us up and seated us in the heavenlies. No longer are we a group of people on earth, but we are a group of people in the heavenlies. In this way, we have entered into life from death and have been transferred from earth to heaven. In this position of resurrection and ascension, we are no longer living in sin; rather, we are walking in the good works that God has prepared for us to walk in (v. 10). In this way, God has worked on us in His grace to such an extent that we have become God's masterpiece.

The word for *masterpiece* in Greek means something that has been made, a handiwork, or something that has been written or composed as a poem. Not only a poetic writing may be considered a poem, but also any work of art that expresses the maker's wisdom and design. God has caused us who were useless ones, sinners dead in sins, to become in the universe something beautiful and expressive of God's wisdom. Before the eyes of the angels, and even before the eyes of the enemy, we are a sweet, beautiful, and wise poem written by God. In other words, we who were useless and were dead in sin have become, through God's grace of life, a song that is singable and enjoyable.

Formerly we were hopeless ones. But God has dispensed His life to us. When this life comes, grace comes as well. The coming of God's grace was a living breath that was breathed into our dead heart, and we were enlivened within. We became alive together with Christ. We also stood up with Christ and became able to move and work. Not only so, God has lifted us to the heavenlies and has seated us in the heavenlies. While we are seated in the heavenlies, God and the angels consider us a beautiful poem. This shows us the extent to which God's dispensing has worked on us.

In ourselves, we do not have the capacity to make ourselves alive, to stand up, and to ascend into the heavens. Our nature does not have the capacity to overcome the power of gravity. However, God's breath of life, His grace of life, has been breathed into us. This grace of life contains a capacity that enables us to ascend until we arrive in the heavenlies, where God is. It has also seated us there so that God might display in the ages which are coming, that is, in the millennium and in the new heaven and new earth, the riches of His grace of life. There we will be as a musical hymn for all creation to sing of God's sweetness, wisdom, and glory. *Hymns*, #203 is a very sweet hymn. As we sing such a hymn, we sense its sweetness and its beauty. I believe that one day, in the kingdom, all the angels will take the lead in the creation to sing such a song of praise to God concerning us as God's poem, God's masterpiece.

THE DIVINE DISPENSING OF GOD THE SON CREATING THE JEWISH AND GENTILE BELIEVERS INTO ONE NEW MAN, THROUGH HIS DEATH ON THE CROSS AND WITH HIS DIVINE ELEMENT, FOR GOD TO ACCOMPLISH HIS DIVINE ECONOMY

Paul went on to show us that before we were saved, we were not only dead, but uncircumcised. In the eyes of the circumcised Jews, we, the uncircumcised Gentiles, were defiled and unclean, like swine and like dogs. We were separated from God's chosen people and from the covenants of God's promise, we were without Christ, and we had no hope and were without God (Eph. 2:11-12). However, Christ came and brought all of us poor people to the cross, so that in His all-inclusive death, the chosen Jews and the chosen Gentiles all died there. The circumcised Jews and the uncircumcised Gentiles were all crucified there. After such an all-inclusive crucifixion, the distinction between the Jews and the Gentiles was removed.

After this, Christ resurrected from the dead. This can be illustrated by a grain of wheat. When it is planted into the earth, on one hand it dies. But on the other hand, it continues to work in death. When Christ was crucified on the cross, in a superficial sense, He died. But actually He was working to

release the divine life. When the divine life was fully manifested, that was resurrection. Hence, resurrection is in fact a
process. In this process, Christ passed through death, and
through His work of death the divine life encased in His
human shell was released. When the Lord was on the cross,
on the one hand, He was dying there, but on the other hand,
His death was His work. At the end of His work on the cross,
the Lord said, "It is finished!" (John 19:30). This means that
in the six hours prior to that time, the Lord had been working.

Even after He died, in Hades the Lord was still working.
After His work in Hades was completed, He walked out of
Hades and told death and Hades goodbye. He did not run away
from death and Hades; rather, He walked out of death and
Hades and entered into resurrection. Through His death
and resurrection, the Lord accomplished one work, which was
to create the chosen Jews and the chosen Gentiles, in Himself,
into one new man (Eph. 2:15). Hence, this work of death and
resurrection was a creating work. On one hand, God's coming
to us in the life of His Son, breathing into us a breath, enlivening us, the dead ones, raising us up together, and seating us
together in the heavenlies in Christ, has made us a universal
poem and God's masterpiece to be sung by the angels to
the praise of God. On the other hand, God's masterpiece also
became a new man created through Christ's death and resurrection. On the cross Christ dealt with His chosen Jews and
chosen Gentiles. He also used death as a process through
which, with His own element, He created all of us in Himself
into one new man so that we can bear remaining fruit and so
that the Body of Christ can propagate continually to be an
expanding church and an expanding Body to accomplish
God's eternal economy on earth. In this new man there is no
more distinction between the Jews and the Gentiles (Col.
3:10-11). This new man causes all of us, the Jewish and the
Gentile believers, to be fully reconciled to God in one Body
and to enjoy Christ as the peace among us and between us and
God (Eph. 2:16-17). Now we, the Jewish and the Gentile
believers, have no problem with each other, and we have no

problem with God. We are together in the church, the Body of Christ, accomplishing God's eternal economy.

IN GOD THE SPIRIT THE TWO GROUPS
THAT COMPOSE THE NEW MAN HAVING ACCESS
UNTO GOD THE FATHER

At the end of Ephesians 2 Paul continued by showing us that the divine dispensing of God the Spirit enables both groups that compose the new man to have access in Him unto God the Father. This causes the Body as the new man to become the kingdom of the Triune God for His administration, the house of God for the dispensing of His love, and the dwelling place of God in the believers' spirit for His rest (vv. 18-22).

In the previous sections, it was God the Father and God the Son coming to us. Beginning from 2:18, we have God the Spirit bringing us to have access unto God the Father for a continual receiving of the dispensing.

God has dispensed Himself to us so that we who were dead in sin could become God's masterpiece, and so that we, the separated ones who were dogs and swine, could become the new man. Now, in the Spirit we have come unto the Father so that daily, moment by moment, we might receive from the Father as the source the continual dispensing. When we enter into Him, fellowship with Him, live before Him, and wait on Him, He gives Himself to us bit by bit as our grace. This bit by bit giving of Himself to us as grace is a continual and eternal dispensing.

Today we are before God. We have been made into a poem by God the Father, created into a new man by God the Son, and brought by God the Spirit unto the Father. There is no longer any separation between us and the Father. This is like a house which already has electricity installed in it. Electricity from the power station can now continually and steadily flow into the house. As we remain in the Father's presence, He continually graces us. This means that continually and eternally we will enjoy His dispensing. It is in this continual dispensing that we all, even as Japanese, Chinese, Koreans, Europeans, and Americans, are coordinated together and are built together. In such a situation, we become, first, God's kingdom, where God exercises His administration. Second, we become a house, a household, of love in which God dispenses His love. Third, this kingdom and this house are God's habitation for His rest. This is the church, and this is all accomplished through God's dispensing.

Dear brothers and sisters, I believe that in these years God will complete His work. In His recovery, God wants us to come up to this standard. You and I, irrespective of our race or color, will not only be the same and love each other, but before the Father, and in this continual, eternal, stable, and steady dispensing, we will even be joined together and coordinated together. Today in the Lord's recovery, we can see a little bit of this situation. We are receiving grace daily in this continual dispensing. The more we receive grace, the more we will be joined, coordinated, and even built together. Thus, we become on earth a kingdom for God to exercise His administration, a household in which He can dispense His love, and a dwelling place of God for His rest. This is Ephesians 2: the Father dispensing life to produce the masterpiece, the Son dispensing through His process of death and resurrection to produce the new man, and the Spirit bringing those who have received grace to come to the Father in one Body, living in God's eternal dispensing. The result is that the church is built up on earth, and God's eternal economy is fulfilled. This is what we hope to see.

(A message given by Brother Witness Lee in Petaling Jaya, Malaysia on November 4, 1990)

Chapter Thirteen

THE DIVINE DISPENSING OF GOD'S PLAN IN HIS ECONOMY AND OF THE APOSTLE'S STEWARDSHIP MINISTERING THE RICHES OF CHRIST TO THE BELIEVERS AND BRINGING IN THE CHURCH FOR THE MANIFESTATION OF GOD'S MULTIFARIOUS WISDOM

OUTLINE AND SCRIPTURE READING

I. The divine dispensing of God's plan in His economy (dispensation) preaching to the Gentiles the unsearchable riches of Christ as the gospel:

    A. To bring to light what is the economy (dispensation) of the mystery, which from the ages has been hidden in God, who created all things.

    B. To bring in the church for the manifestation of God's multifarious wisdom to the rulers and authorities in the heavenlies—Eph. 3:8-10.

Ephesians 3:8-10

To me, less than the least of all saints, was this grace given, to preach to the nations the unsearchable riches of Christ as the gospel, (9) and to bring to light what is the dispensation of the mystery, which from the ages has been hidden in God, who created all things; (10) in order that now to the rulers and the authorities in the heavenlies might be made known through the church the multifarious wisdom of God.

II. **The divine dispensing of the apostle's stewardship ministering to the Gentile believers the
riches of Christ as God's grace, that:**

A. **The mystery of Christ—the church—may be
manifested.**

B. **The Gentile believers may become joint heirs
and a joint Body and joint partakers of God's
promise in Christ—Eph. 3:2-6.**

Ephesians 3:2-6
If indeed you have heard of the stewardship of
the grace of God which was given to me for you,
(3) that by revelation the mystery was made
known to me, as I have written previously in
brief, (4) by which, in reading it, you can per-
ceive my understanding in the mystery of Christ,
(5) which in other generations was not made
known to the sons of men, as it has now been
revealed to His holy apostles and prophets in
spirit, (6) that the nations are to be joint heirs
and a joint Body and joint partakers of the
promise in Christ Jesus through the gospel.

III. **The apostle's stewardship perfecting the saints
unto the work of the New Testament minis-
try—the building up of the Body of Christ—Eph.
4:11-12.**

Ephesians 4:11-12
And He gave some apostles, and some prophets,
and some evangelists, and some shepherds and
teachers, (12) for the perfecting of the saints unto
the work of ministry, unto the building up of the
Body of Christ.

The apostle Paul wrote the book of Ephesians in a very meaningful way. In chapter one he shows us how the Body of Christ is produced and exists out of the dispensing of the Triune God. Then, in chapter two he begins from another angle to show us the history of those who have been worked on by God's dispensing to become the Body of Christ. With that as the background, he shows us that the church, a precious thing that was produced out of God's dispensing, is a masterpiece, a most beautiful poem in the universe that the angels love to sing. Whenever the angels see a sinner saved, they sing. When they see the church, they will surely sing all the more. Then Paul shows us that in Christ's death and resurrection, He used His divine element as the material to produce a universal new man. Finally, this masterpiece, this new man that can accomplish God's eternal economy, is brought to God in one Spirit, having drawn near to God, without any barrier whatsoever, and remains in the presence of God to receive God's continual and eternal dispensing. Like a steady stream, God dispenses Himself little by little into those who have a part in this new man. It is this continual, steady, eternal dispensing that coordinates them together, constitutes them together, and builds them up together. This built-up church is God's kingdom on earth for the executing of His administration. It is also the household for the dispensing of His love, and as such, it becomes His eternal habitation in our spirit. After reading the first two chapters we should have a clear view concerning the church.

THE EXECUTION OF THE DIVINE DISPENSING

In chapter three Paul goes on to show us from another angle how God's dispensing is executed and carried out. He speaks of God's mystery in eternity, and this mystery is His economy. God's dispensing is fully something that is in His economy, something in His plan, something in His purpose and arrangement. In order to carry out this dispensing and for the execution of this dispensing, the Triune God selected some with whom He was pleased, and whom He could use, and made them His dispensers, richly bestowing upon them His grace. Through God's rich grace, there was an operation of God's power within these people. These apostles and prophets then fulfilled their ministry according to the operation of God. Under such circumstances, the ministry of these ones is called the stewardship. They are the stewards because they are there to execute God's dispensing.

In Greek the word for *economy* (*oikonomia*) denotes a household law, a household administration. The function of such a household administration is to manage all the riches of the household so that these riches will be distributed to the family members and that the lord of the house would be satisfied and have his desires fulfilled. In order to accomplish this, God has arranged to have many apostles and prophets to be stewards in His household management to manage the distribution of the riches of His great family, so that all the members of His family, that is, those who have a part in this family, will be able to share in the riches of God's great household and thus satisfy His desire.

The apostle Paul was indeed such a steward. He exercised his stewardship to dispense God's rich grace, that is, the unsearchable riches of Christ, to others. Hence, Paul's stewardship is the execution of God's economy. In 3:9 the word *oikonomia* is translated *dispensation* (*economy*), whereas in 3:2 it is translated *stewardship*. It is the same word, *oikonomia*. But it is translated differently. God's economy, God's universal household administration, is to distribute God's unlimited riches in Christ. Paul said that he received a special commission, a special grace, and a special operation to transmit the unsearchable riches of Christ to the Gentiles chosen by God. This was his stewardship. Hence, the stewardship is God's economy. The execution of God's economy depends on the stewardship. Without the stewardship God has no way to execute His economy. The church is built on the foundation of the apostles and prophets. This means that it is built on the revelation and the vision that they saw. This is similar to what the Lord Jesus said in Matthew 16:18. He would build His church upon "this rock." That rock is not mainly the rock itself, but the revelation concerning the rock. Peter told the Lord, "You are the Christ, the Son of the living God." That revelation became the foundation of the building up of the church. The revelation and vision that the apostles saw is the foundation for the building up of the church. Upon this foundation are built all the riches of Christ. These are the unsearchable riches of Christ. The unsearchable riches of Christ are the unlimited grace of God. However, these riches, that is this grace, are not the direct material for the building; it must first be embodied in the individual believers, making these improper and useless believers the materials for the building up of the church.

THE RESULT OF THE DIVINE DISPENSING

For this reason, there must be a process of transformation. First Corinthians 3 reveals that the believers originally are plants, but through the process of transformation by the riches of Christ and by His life, these plants become minerals. They are transformed from plants to be gold, silver, and precious stones. According to the scriptural principle, precious materials are not created but are transformed from some previous elements. This process of transformation is a process of dispensing. The apostle Paul and his co-workers bore the responsibility to be the stewards in God's great family to execute this dispensing which dispenses the riches of the great household, that is, the riches of Christ, bit by bit to all of us. This dispensing was given to those in the ancient times as well as to those in this age. After we enjoy all these riches, these riches produce a transformation within us. Paul has also used this term in one of his other epistles, which says, "And do not be conformed to this age, but be transformed by the renewing of the mind" (Rom. 12:2). We must be transformed from wood, grass, and stubble to gold, silver, and precious stones before we are qualified to be the materials for the building up of the church. Paul warned us that the foundation is laid, and that other foundation no one is able to lay. But when we build upon this foundation, we have to take heed with what materials we build. Do we build with wood, grass, and stubble, or with gold, silver, and precious stones? If there is not much gold, silver, or precious stones, but much wood, grass, and stubble, the judgment day will come and the Lord's judging fire will be a test as to which parts will remain and which parts will be burned (1 Cor. 3:10-15). Paul said clearly in 1 Corinthians 3 that the work of some shall be consumed. But this does not mean that these ones will perish. We are not saved by our works, but by the redemption of the Lord. However, if one's work is consumed, his salvation will be one that is "as through fire." What will remain are the gold, silver, and precious stones. Gold refers to the Father's nature, silver refers to the Son's redemption, and precious stones refer to the transformation of the Spirit, which produces precious stones. Hence, to use gold, silver, and precious stones for the building of the church is to use the Triune God as the element for building. Today the Triune God is embodied in Christ. All the fullness dwells in Christ bodily. What we have received from the apostles is a divine dispensing, which dispenses all the divine riches in Christ into us. Tonight, while we come to God's Word, we are receiving the dispensing of this word, which dispenses the riches of the divine element of Christ into us. Within this dispensing is holiness, righteousness, redemption, and many other things. This is clearly revealed in the New Testament.

At the end of the New Testament, we see the coming New Jerusalem. The entire city proper bears the golden nature of God. It is a golden city built upon a golden hill. The twelve gates are twelve pearls, which refer to the dispensing of life in the death and resurrection of Christ. This can be seen from the way the oyster produces the pearls. When an oyster is wounded by a piece of sand, it secretes its life element around the sand, eventually producing a pearl. This typifies Christ secreting His life in resurrection to embrace us, making us the pearls. The wall of the New Jerusalem on four sides is built with jasper, which has the same appearance as God. Thus, the city fully transmits God's glory and expresses God's image. Such a city concludes the revelation concerning Christ in the Bible, and especially that in the New Testament. This Christ is ultimately enlarged and expanded to become a city. This enlargement and expansion is the church. The church is His enlargement, continuation, and completion. When we see and understand the New Jerusalem, we will realize that the result of the stewardship of the apostles in dispensing the riches of Christ is the church. The ultimate consummation of this church is the New Jerusalem. This is the dispensing that we are speaking of here.

THE DIVINE DISPENSING
OF THE APOSTLES' STEWARDSHIP

The dispensing began with God's economy. Before the ages God, in the universe, had a desire in Himself, which was to work Himself into His chosen, created, redeemed, and regenerated people that He might be their life and their divine element. Although they are human, these people are born of God to have God's nature and God's life and to thus become God's genuine children. As such, these people become God's expression, and this expression becomes the Body of Christ, which is also the fullness of Christ. This fullness is the riches of the Triune God fully worked into His chosen, regenerated, and transformed people. In order to accomplish this, God in His economy must have an arrangement and a plan, and He must find some faithful and useful ones and entrust this responsibility to them. Among them the most important group are the first apostles. God gave them the stewardship so that they would be responsible to dispense all the riches of Christ to God's children, that is, to the Body of Christ. Paul's fourteen Epistles are a full revelation. They show how Paul and his co-workers carried out the stewardship of distributing the riches of Christ in God's great household through the writing of the fourteen Epistles. These Epistles bring in an unsearchable and ever-fresh dispensing throughout the ages, even until today. Tonight, in this little meeting, what we are doing and touching is this same dispensing. We are gathered into His name, that is, we are in His Spirit. Here we gather around His Word to consider the revelation in the Word, and especially the vision revealed in the fourteen Epistles of Paul. If we see this vision, we will realize that our need is the riches of Christ dispensed to us by Paul. We do not need any spiritual cultivation or any reformation. We only need to receive this divine dispensing from Paul again and again in a slow and steady way from morning to evening and from evening to morning. Practically speaking, Christ in resurrection is the pneumatic Christ. Hence, everywhere and all the time, He can enter into us, be with us, and be our life and our element within.

Most Christians today have left the proper truth and have turned from the inward dispensing of Christ to human work, merits, and religion. We ourselves have been under this influence and are not free from it even up to today. Whenever we read something from the Bible, we make up our mind to do and to fulfill it. However, such determination should be condemned and rejected. God does not want us to determine to do what the Bible says; He only wants us to receive His dispensing.

Here I would like to read to you *Hymns*, #501. This hymn expresses very well what I want to say. Verse 1 says:

> O glorious Christ, Savior mine,
> Thou art truly radiance divine;
> God infinite, in eternity,
> Yet man in time, finite to be.
>
> Oh! Christ, expression of God, the Great,
> Inexhaustible, rich, and sweet!

Such a One is for our enjoyment, and not for our imitation.

> God mingled with humanity
> Lives in me my all to be.

He does not live in us to be our pattern. If that were the case, we would have to do something. Instead He lives in us to be our blessed portion, so that we can enjoy Him. Modern nutritionists tell us that we become what we eat. Americans eat a lot of beef. As a result they even smell like the cow. Whatever we enjoy as our nutrition, we become that very thing. In John 6:57, the Lord Jesus said that he who eats Him will live because of Him. It is those who eat Him, and not those who imitate Him. Those who eat Him are those who enjoy Him. The Lord Jesus is edible and drinkable. Those who eat and drink of Him will have Him within them as their life and life nutrients, and will be able to live by Him. This is God's economy and God's dispensing. This is the goal of the apostle's work on us, that through his epistles, he would transfuse us, strengthen us, and dispense to us bit by bit the Christ whom he experienced, not as our example or even as our power, but as our nutrition. This nutrition eventually becomes our strength. This is not something that results from our work, but from the growth. Verse 2 says:

> The fulness of God dwells in Thee;
> Thou dost manifest God's glory;
> In flesh Thou hast redemption wrought;
> As Spirit, oneness with me sought.

If He had not become the Spirit, He could not be one with us. The New Testament says that he who is joined to the Lord is one spirit with Him. This is possible because in resurrection He has become the life-giving Spirit. Verse 3 says:

> All things of the Father are Thine;
> All Thou art in Spirit is mine;
> The Spirit makes Thee real to me,
> That Thou experienced might be.

It does not say that He will become our pattern, but our experience. His experience is my history. My walk today is a continuation of His history. Verse 4 says:

> The Spirit of life causes Thee
> By Thy Word to transfer to me.
> Thy Spirit touched, Thy word received,
> Thy life in me is thus conceived.

He is not conceived as our standard, but as our supply. Verse 5 says:

> In spirit while gazing on Thee,
> As a glass reflecting Thy glory,
> Like to Thyself transformed I'll be,
> That Thou might be expressed thru me.

This means that we have become His duplication. He is duplicated and lived out from within us. He and we become fully one. He is our life within, and we become His living without. In this way, He is expressed through us. The last verse says:

> Thy Spirit will me saturate,
> Every part will God permeate,
> Deliv'ring me from the old man,
> With all saints building for His plan.

This is to be built up in spirit to become a habitation of God in spirit. This is what God is after, and is what the stewardship of the apostles strives to attain.

I hope that all the brothers and sisters, whether old or young, whether they were saved recently or have served the Lord for a long time, would all see a vision. Today, God has no intention for us to do anything by ourselves. It is true that whatever He wants us to do we should do. But God wants us to do everything by depending on Him, by taking Him as life, and by allowing Him to dispense Himself into us. When we enjoy Him and experience Him, we can express Him. This is what God is after. When you go home, you do not need to make up your mind. All you need to do is to sit quietly before the Lord. You do not need to kneel down. This does not mean that we must not kneel down. It means that to kneel down is not a necessity. If you remain quietly before the Lord, and allow your spirit to reflect within you the light you saw in the last few days, you will realize that what you need and lack is not to do something, but to receive His dispensing day by day. You need to receive the Lord's word every day, and contact His Spirit. In this way, the Lord will become your supply. If you have a bad temper, and are used to losing your temper at your wife and children, you may think, "After listening to these few messages, I feel really shameful. I have been a Christian for twenty-eight years. Today I still get mad at my wife and children. This is to my shame. When I go home, I have to fast for three days and ask the Lord to save me, to have pity on me, and to change my temper. I do not have the strength in myself. I cannot do it. But I am willing to trust in the Lord and to ask Him to change me." I can tell you that this prayer will surely not be answered. This kind of prayer is an insult to God. He wants to enter into you to become you, and to replace you. You have to hand yourself over to Him. He will then give Himself to you. He will live a grafted life with you.

When two trees are grafted together, they do not exchange their lives. Rather, the two lives are mingled as one life, and the two trees are mingled as one tree. Both are living, yet they do not live separately. Rather, they live mutually within one another. The grafted branch lives in the tree and the tree lives in the grafted branch. The two lives become one life, and the two livings become one living. This is the grafted life, and is also the mingled life.

Galatians 2:20 speaks of such a life. After saying, "I have been crucified with Christ, and it is no longer I who live," it says, "But Christ lives in me; and the life which I now live in the flesh I live in faith…." The living which I now live is a living in which Christ is living Himself out from me. It is true that Christ lives, but He lives in us. We need to see clearly that what the Lord desires is that we and He would be mingled as one. The Lord is our person, and we are His expression; the two become one. "But he who is joined to the Lord is one spirit" (1 Cor. 6:17). The center of all of Paul's epistles with their thousands of words and instructions is this: Christ living in us and being expressed through us. We do not need to do or to perform anything. This is the stewardship that Paul received. For the past two thousand years, he has been doing this work of dispensing on earth. Although he is not with us today, his word is still here. Although he has passed away, he is still speaking. Through these speakings, the riches of the pneumatic Christ are dispensed little by little into us. In this way, Christ increases in us, and through this increase we grow in life. In this growth, our self, our natural man, is diminished and annulled, and we are delivered from ourselves and are joined to the saints to be built into God's habitation, which is the church.

THE STEWARDSHIP OF THE APOSTLE IN PERFECTING THE SAINTS UNTO THE WORK OF THE NEW TESTAMENT MINISTRY

Furthermore, in Ephesians 4, Paul tells us that God has an economy. This economy is for the dispensing of His riches in Christ to His chosen ones who have believed in Him. This economy requires a group of people like the apostles for its execution and fulfillment. But do not think that in God's economy the stewardship is only entrusted to the apostles and the prophets and that they alone will accomplish the work. The apostles' stewardship is for the perfecting of the saints unto the work of the New Testament ministry, which is the building up of the Body of Christ. If there are some among us who have received this grace to have the apostles' steward-ship, they must remember that they are not here to do everything by themselves. They should learn of the apostle Paul. Paul says that the Head has given gifts to the Body, such as the apostles, prophets, evangelists, and shepherds and teachers. These people are for the perfecting of the saints, that is, for the dispensing of Christ to the other saints, perfecting them to an extent that they may do the work of the New Testament ministry, which is to directly build up the Body of Christ.

Suppose there are three hundred fifty saints meeting here, and we have the church services. I am concerned that all that you understand as church service is just the cleaning of the floor, the washing of the windows, the ushering, etc. Let me ask you, can these be considered the church services? This is difficult to answer. I would like to consider with you if in these business affairs we are distributing Christ to others. In principle, only one thing counts in the church service, which is the distributing of Christ to others. To preach the gospel and to bring people to salvation is definitely to distribute Christ to others. That is surely a church service. After people are saved, they become the new believers, the lambs. We have to feed the lambs. This feeding of the lambs after the gospel preaching is also a distribution of Christ to others. After this, we have to continue to lead them. Not only do we have to feed them for two or three months; we may have to spend a year or two years to care for them. Not only do we have to care for them in private, but we also have to bring them to the meetings. This is also to distribute Christ to them. First Corinthians 14 also teaches us that when the whole church comes together, everyone should have something to present to others. This is not the so-called "worship service" in Chris-tianity, but a meeting in which everyone has something to present. Paul says that we can all prophesy, that is, to speak for God, to speak forth God, and to speak God into others one by one. Hence, whenever we come together as the church, everyone has to learn to speak for the Lord. What we see today in Christianity as the Lord's Day morning worship service is a totally unscriptural practice. The Bible tells us that when the whole church comes together, everyone should have something to present. In other words, everyone should have something to say. To run errands and to manage affairs is not service. In type, those are not the work of the priests, but the work of the Levites, the miscellaneous works. The work of the priest is to offer sacrifices, to light the lamps, and to burn incense. Is there a priest who does not offer sacrifices? If one does not offer sacrifices, he is not a priest. Today in the church service, we must be able to distribute Christ to others. In the meeting, all you have to do is to say in a proper way: "Christ is my life. He is living a temper-killing life within me. I can never control my temper by myself. Even if I can do it, it does not count in God's eyes. What God wants is to have Christ live out of me." For you to speak these few words is for you to minister Christ. But today we have been influenced by our background and environment. We have the wrong concept that on Sunday, we have to either speak a long message, or not say anything. In the end, the more some do not speak, the more they become unable to speak. We must create an atmosphere among us that encourages everyone to speak. If you cannot speak a lot, speak a little. If you cannot speak three sentences, speak one sentence. I say this to make you clear that the church service is to minister Christ to others. For this reason, at the beginning of chapter three Paul said that he received a special grace; God gave to him the stewardship of grace that he might minister and dispense God's grace to others. By chapter four, he went on further to describe what the Head has given to the church—the apostles, the prophets, the evangelists, the shepherds and teachers. All these are for the perfecting of the saints, so that all the saints can participate in the building up of the Body of Christ, the very work that the apostles are entrusted with. In this way, does it not mean that after being perfected, every saint in the church becomes an apostle? Do you believe that everyone in the church can minister Christ, and that every sister among you can more or less minister Christ and can dispense Christ to others? The answer is definitely yes. Hence, we can all build up the Body of Christ. All those who build up the Body of Christ are either apostles, prophets, evangelists, or shepherds and teachers. In this way, all of us become these people. We will all become the apostles, the prophets, the evangelists, the shepherds and teachers.

God's dispensing is for the fulfillment of His eternal plan, which is the building up of the church as His Body and habitation on earth. This is fully a matter of the divine dispensing. This dispensing in His economy is on three levels. First, God in His economy does the dispensing Himself in producing the apostles, the prophets, the evangelists, and the shepherds and teachers. Second, these gifted ones fulfill their ministry by perfecting the other saints. Third, the perfected saints do the work of the apostles and the prophets, that is, the work of the New Testament ministry, which is the building up of the Body of Christ. In this way the dispensing of God can reach its ultimate goal—the building up of the Body of Christ.

(A message given by Brother Witness Lee in Petaling Jaya, Malaysia on November 4, 1990)

THE DIVINE DISPENSING
OF THE ALL-INCLUSIVE CHRIST
IN HIS MAKING HIS HOME IN
THE BELIEVERS' HEARTS
SUPPLYING TO THE SAINTS
THE FULLNESS OF THE TRIUNE GOD
THAT THE CHURCH MAY BECOME
THE FULL EXPRESSION OF THE TRIUNE GOD

OUTLINE AND SCRIPTURE READING

I. The divine dispensing of God the Father strengthening the believers with power, according to the riches of His glory, through His Spirit into the inner man that the believers may experience and enjoy:

   A. The dispensing of the riches of the glory of God the Father.

   B. The dispensing of the operation of the Spirit of God the Father.

   C. The dispensing of the strengthening with the divine power—Eph. 3:14-16.

   Ephesians 3:14-16
   For this cause I bow my knees unto the Father, (15) of whom every family in the heavens and on earth is named, (16) that He would grant you, according to the riches of His glory, to be strengthened with power through His Spirit into the inner man.

II. The divine dispensing of Christ in His making His home in the believers' hearts through faith, that the believers:

A. Being rooted for growth and grounded for building up in love.

B. May be strong to apprehend with all the saints the breadth and length and height and depth of the universe, which are the immeasurable dimensions of Christ.

C. And to know and experience the divine dispensing of the knowledge-surpassing love of Christ.

D. That they may be filled unto all the fullness of God to be the corporate expression of the Triune God—Eph. 3:17-19.

Ephesians 3:17-19
That Christ may make His home in your hearts through faith, that you, having been rooted and grounded in love, (18) may be strong to apprehend with all the saints what is the breadth and length and height and depth, (19) and to know the knowledge-surpassing love of Christ, that you may be filled unto all the fullness of God.

GOD'S ECONOMY BECOMING
THE APOSTLES' STEWARDSHIP

As we have seen, depending on the context, the Greek word *oikonomia* can be translated either *economy* (or, *dispensation*) or *stewardship*. In God it is a plan, a purpose, and an economy, but when God's economy comes to the apostles, it becomes a stewardship.

God's economy is a great matter. It includes, first, the creation of the heavens, the earth, and all living creatures to produce the old creation. The work of producing the old creation was done by God Himself alone. But when God comes in to produce the new creation, He works through the principle of incarnation. In other words, He cooperates with man and needs man's cooperation. God has everything in Himself. But in the new creation, He must have man's cooperation before He can produce anything. He needs man to become one life and one spirit with Him and to be joined and mingled with Him, before the new creation can be realized. God must mingle Himself with man in order to realize the new creation. God's economy is a great matter. In order to carry out such an economy, God must have stewards to serve, to minister, to manage, and to execute His economy. First, this stewardship was entrusted to the apostles. God entrusted His economy to the apostles. When the apostles took up God's economy, it became a ministry, a stewardship, in them. Our concept may be that only the apostles and other gifted ones are worthy to bear the stewardship of God's economy and that we, the "small potatoes," are worthy only to do the cleaning and the ushering work but are unworthy to bear such a stewardship. However, in the light of the New Testament teaching, all the believers are priests, whether Paul or Peter or any other brothers or sisters, old or young (1 Pet. 2:5, 9; Rev. 1:5-6). Thus, God's economy has become the stewardship of all the believers. The apostle Paul and we bear the same stewardship. Although his stewardship may have been greater, he was still just a steward. We are also stewards, being on the same level as he was.

THE GIFTED ONES PERFECTING THE SAINTS
UNTO THE WORK OF THE NEW TESTAMENT MINISTRY

Ephesians 4:11 shows us the Head giving all kinds of gifts in ascension. These gifts include the apostles, prophets, evangelists, and shepherds and teachers. In verse 12 there is a sixth title—the saints. The gifted ones mentioned earlier are not there for themselves but for the perfecting of the saints. The saints are not for the apostles. Rather, the apostles are for the saints. If the saints are for the apostles, the same mistake as that committed by the Corinthians will happen. Some will say that they are of Paul, while others will say that they are of Apollos, and there will be division among us (1 Cor. 1:12). This is why Paul said that the saints were not for him, but that he was for the saints. They do not belong to Paul. Rather, Paul belongs to them, because all things are theirs, whether the world, or life, or death, or things present, or things to come, all are theirs (1 Cor. 3:21-22). The saints are the "princes," the ones who will inherit the earth (Rom. 4:13). The apostles are the slaves of the saints. The apostles, prophets, and evangelists are all there to perfect the saints and are all slaves (2 Cor. 4:5). Furthermore, the goal of the apostles and the prophets, as the gifted ones serving the saints, is to enable everyone to do the work of the New Testament ministry, which is the building up of the Body of Christ. Every saint can do the work of an apostle, a prophet, an evangelist, a shepherd and a teacher. This is the difference between the God-ordained way in the Bible and the traditional way of Christianity. The way of Christianity is for the minority, the clergy, to become more and more able, while the rest of the saints become the laity; they have been laid off, and are there only for the worshipping services. To put it not so nicely, they have all been written off. This is something God hates (Rev. 2:6). Although we have come out of the denominations and the sects to practice the Lord's recovery, unfortunately we have not rid ourselves fully of some of the germs and poison of the denominations and the sects. Yet we are not aware of this. We may still hold the concept that the apostles, prophets, evangelists, and shepherds and teachers, and also the elders, are the able ones and are of a higher rank than the rest of the saints. However, the word of the Lord says that among us there is no distinction of being high or low, great or small. Every one is a brother. If anyone wants to be great, he has to be the slave to everyone. The elders are the head sheep among the flock. They should even take the lead to clean the toilets. They should not stand on the side, ordering others to work. Among us we should not have any concept of a hierarchy. The Bible says that we all are members of the Body of Christ (1 Cor. 12:27; Eph. 5:30). Since we are members, we all have a function. The Bible also says that we all are priests, and we can all offer spiritual sacrifices, light the lamps, and burn the incense. Everyone can do these things. Whatever the apostles, the prophets, the evangelists, and the shepherds and teachers can do, they should teach, train, and perfect us so that every one of us will be able to do the same, perhaps even better.

The Lord's "new way" today is that the gifted ones would perfect those who are not gifted, so that, after a period of time, they all will become gifted. In the first year of his study in the university, a student is inferior to his professors. But after passing through four years of university study, two years of graduate school, and three years of a Ph.D. program, a student will become a Ph.D., and may become better than his professors. We need to see that the service in the church, on one hand, is to supply Christ to others, and on the other hand, to perfect others. After we perfect others, the perfected ones will be able to do the same work that we can do, and perhaps they will do it even better. This is the standard that the Bible has set for us. We need to find a way by all means to realize Ephesians 4:11-12. If all the brothers and sisters among us are perfected and can minister Christ for the building up of the church, what an increase the church will experience! After a person is saved and helped by us for four years, he should be able to participate in all aspects of service; he should be able to preach the gospel to minister Christ for others' salvation; he should be able to shepherd the new believers as the lambs in the church; he should be able to teach and perfect them in the group meetings, and he should be able to gradually help them to prophesy and speak for the

Lord for the building up of the church. These are the four steps of our new way: the begetting, the nourishing, the teaching, and the building. Eventually when we come to the meetings, we will not need to look to the preachers. Every attendant will be able to speak for the Lord. The meetings will become very fresh, living, and rich.

EXAMPLES OF THE APOSTLES
PERFECTED TO BE THE MINISTERS

In chapters one, three, and four of 2 Corinthians, Paul described how he and the other apostles became dispensers of Christ. He used at least four illustrations to describe how the apostles pursued and grew. First, in 1:21 Paul said that the apostles had been anointed by God. The anointing ointment symbolizes the ultimate consummation of the Triune God, who as the ointment of the compound Spirit anoints us. The more this Spirit anoints us, the more we gain the element of God. Second, in 1:22 Paul said that this Spirit had also sealed the apostles. This means that after they were sealed, they were continually saturated, permeated, and filled with the Spirit. Then, in 3:18 Paul said that the apostles were like mirrors who, with unveiled face, beheld and reflected the Lord's glorious image, and fellowshipped with the Lord face to face. They did not behold only once and then go away. They beheld repeatedly. In this way, the Lord's glorious image was reflected on these mirrors and they were gradually being transformed into that glorious image by the Lord Spirit. Finally, in 4:7-16 Paul said that the apostles were earthen vessels with Christ as the treasure within, through whom they received the excellency of God's great power and were able to experience the daily putting to death of their outward man so that the treasure within could daily radiate and be magnified from within. As such persons they became ministers who were able to minister Christ, transmit Him, and dispense Him to others. They were also able to fully execute God's economy through their ministry, which is the preaching and ministering of the unsearchable riches of Christ for the producing of the church. In this way, they fulfilled God's economy. If these apostles as the perfecting ones are such persons who would be learning all the time, those whom they perfect and help should become the same as they are, learning all the time also. Thus, in the churches of the Lord's recovery we need to create an atmosphere in which the gifted ones constantly do the work of perfecting the saints. They should take every opportunity to perfect others. At the same time, all the saints are constantly learning. In the end, every saint in the church will be able to speak for the Lord, to preach the gospel, to shepherd and perfect others. Everyone will be a priest, and will be able to carry out the stewardship for the execution of God's New Testament economy. This is what the Lord is after today.

THE DIVINE DISPENSING OF GOD THE FATHER STRENGTHENING THE BELIEVERS WITH POWER, ACCORDING TO THE RICHES OF HIS GLORY, THROUGH HIS SPIRIT INTO THE INNER MAN

The apostle Paul was very capable of doing the work of perfecting the saints. In Ephesians 3 he shows us how he taught and perfected others. First, he prayed for all the saints whom he perfected. He bowed his knees to the Father and prayed that the Father would strengthen the saints with power through His Spirit into the inner man. The power with which the Father strengthens the saints is the power that enabled the Lord Jesus to resurrect from the dead, to ascend to the heavens, and to become the Lord and Christ. Whether our spiritual life is proper or not depends on our inner man, which is our regenerated spirit. There is a hymn that says: "The Spirit begets the spirit; the spirit worships the Spirit, so that we are filled with the Spirit. The Spirit becomes the word, and with the abundant life, flows as the river of living water." This hymn conveys the thought in John 3, 4, 6, and 7. John 3:6 says that our spirit is begotten of the Spirit: "That which is born of the Spirit is spirit." John 4:24 says that our spirit worships the Spirit: "God is Spirit; and those who worship Him must worship in spirit…." By such worshipping, we are filled with the Spirit. John 6:63 says that the Spirit becomes the word: "The words which I have spoken unto you are spirit and are life." Then John 7:38 says that with this

Spirit, there is the abundant life flowing as rivers of living water. The more one sings this hymn, the more he will become living, and the more his inner man will be strengthened.

THE DIVINE DISPENSING OF CHRIST IN MAKING HIS HOME IN THE BELIEVERS' HEARTS THROUGH FAITH

When our inner man is strengthened, spontaneously we will be open to the Lord, and Christ will be able to make home in our hearts through faith. To make home is to settle down. It is not to be a guest or a temporary boarder. The Lord is often like a guest within us; He cannot settle down. Although we love the Lord, in our mind there are still corners which the Lord cannot touch, in the will there are still parts that have not yielded to the Lord, and in the emotions there are still other loves that block the Lord from entering in. Because of this, the Lord cannot do anything. Paul's prayer was for us to be strengthened in our spirit, so that the Lord could gain every part and could settle down in our hearts. Our heart is like a house with a few rooms. It has the mind, the will, the emotion, and the conscience. When our spirit is strong, we will allow the Lord to occupy and to fill every part. The Lord will then be able to make home in our whole being comfortably and properly.

In Love Being Rooted for Growth and Grounded for Building Up

When Christ makes home in our hearts, in His love we can be rooted for growth and grounded for building up (Eph. 3:17). When we are rooted and grounded in the Lord's love this way, we will be able to receive the Lord's inward dispensing again and again. When the Lord makes home within us, He will spread within us, and His spreading will be His dispensing. The more He spreads Himself, the more He will dispense Himself to us. When He spreads to our mind, emotion, will, and even to our conscience, all our inward parts will receive more of His dispensing. More and more we will realize the Lord as the lovable One, and will be rooted and grounded in His love. In this way, we can be an apostle as Paul was. Paul's prayer can be considered as a prayer for the saints to become the apostles. Throughout the ages, countless numbers of saints have been perfected by his prayer.

Being Strong to Apprehend with All the Saints the Breadth and Length and Height and Depth of the Universe, Which Are the Immeasurable Dimensions of Christ

When we are rooted and grounded in Christ's love, we will be full of power and strength to comprehend with all the saints the breadth and length and height and depth of the universe, which are the immeasurable dimensions of Christ. There are these four dimensions in the universe, the breadth, the length, the height, and the depth. But no one can say how broad is the breadth, how long the length, how high the height, or how deep the depth. These immeasurable dimensions are the dimensions of Christ. The more we are rooted and grounded in His love, experience and enjoy His love, the more we will comprehend with all the saints His immeasurableness. This proves not only that we have received His dispensing, but that we have received it immeasurably. The more we receive Him, the more immeasurable and unlimited He becomes, and the more we realize that He is immeasurable and His riches are unsearchable.

Knowing and Experiencing the Divine Dispensing of the Knowledge-surpassing Love of Christ, to Be Filled unto All the Fullness of God to Be the Corporate Expression of the Triune God

After we are rooted and grounded, and have become strong to comprehend the immeasurable dimensions of Christ and to enjoy and experience the divine dispensing of His knowledge-surpassing love, our whole being will be filled unto all the fullness of God, and we will become the corporate expression of the processed Triune God. If all of us are like this, surely we all will be perfected to become apostles and prophets.

In these verses Paul shows us how he perfects the saints until every one of them becomes the same as he was. He was a person who experienced Christ; he was strong in spirit, and the Lord could make His home in every part of his heart.

He was full of the sweetness of Christ, full of His love, and experienced all His dimensions. Since he was such an apostle, his perfecting will make us the same as he was. In this way, the souls are saved, the sheep are led back to the flock, and all the saints are perfected to be the gifted ones to do the work of the New Testament ministry, which is the building up of the Body of Christ for the fulfillment of God's eternal economy.

(A message given by Brother Witness Lee in Petaling Jaya, Malaysia on November 5, 1990)

CHAPTER FIFTEEN

THE DIVINE DISPENSING
OF THE DIVINE TRINITY
CONSTITUTING THE GIFTS FOR
THE PERFECTING OF THE SAINTS
UNTO THE BUILDING UP OF
THE ORGANIC BODY OF CHRIST

OUTLINE AND SCRIPTURE READING

I. The divine dispensing of the Spirit as the essence of the Body of Christ causing all the members of the Body of Christ to have one hope of glory, which is the redemption of their bodies, that their whole being may enter into the divine glory—Eph. 4:4.

Ephesians 4:4
One Body and one Spirit, as also you were called in one hope of your calling.

II. The divine dispensing of the Lord as the element of His Body causing all His members:

A. To have a life-union with Him in His divine element through faith.

B. And to have a separating transfer out of Adam and the Adamic world through baptism—Eph. 4:5.

Ephesians 4:5
One Lord, one faith, one baptism.

III. The divine dispensing of God the Father to the Body of Christ in His being over all, as the Father's overshadowing, in His being through all, as the Son's care and concern, and in

His being in all, as the Spirit's presence, enabling all the members of the Body of Christ to experience the Triune God and enjoy His rich presence—Eph. 4:6.

Ephesians 4:6
One God and Father of all, who is over all and through all and in all.

IV. The divine dispensing of the One who descended into Hades, who was raised, and who ascended to the heavens, that is, the resurrected and ascended Head, Christ, constituting His many gifts and making these gifts:

A. The gifts He gave to His Body.

B. Who also perfect the saints through the divine dispensing that all the saints:

  1. May be able to do the work of the New Testament ministry, which is the building up of the organic Body of Christ.

  2. That all the members of the Body of Christ may grow up into the Head, Christ, in all things:

    a. And out from the Head receiving the dispensing of His rich supply.

    b. Through every joint of the rich supply, joining the Body closely together.

    c. And through the operation in measure of each one part, fitly knitting the Body together.

    d. Causing the growth of the Body unto the building up of itself in love—Eph. 4:8-16.

Ephesians 4:8-16
Wherefore He says, Having ascended to the height, He led captive those taken captive and gave gifts to men. (9) (Now this, He ascended, what is it except that He also descended into the lower parts of the earth? (10) He who descended is the

same who also ascended far above all the heavens that He might fill all things.) (11) And He gave some apostles, and some prophets, and some evangelists, and some shepherds and teachers, (12) for the perfecting of the saints unto the work of ministry, unto the building up of the Body of Christ; (13) until we all arrive at the oneness of the faith and of the full knowledge of the Son of God, at a full-grown man, at the measure of the stature of the fullness of Christ, (14) that we may be no longer babes tossed by waves and carried about by every wind of teaching in the sleight of men, in craftiness with a view to a system of error; (15) but holding to truth in love, we may grow up into Him in all things, who is the Head, Christ, (16) out from whom all the Body, fitted and knit together through every joint of the supply, according to the operation in measure of each one part, causes the growth of the Body unto the building up of itself in love.

From Ephesians chapters one, two, and three, we have seen one vision after another. These visions conclude with all the riches of God, which can be considered as the peak. However, this is only the first half of the book. After these chapters, there are still chapters four, five, and six. Now, from chapter four, we will consider the divine dispensing in the divine economy from another angle. This angle is very high, particular, and practical. It shows us that the divine dispensing begins with the Triune God and ends with us, the believers. This is very meaningful.

In Ephesians 4:4-6, Paul first refers to the one Body, the one Spirit, and the one hope of our calling. Then he refers to the one Lord, the one faith, and the one baptism. Finally, he refers to the one God and Father of all, who is over all and through all and in all. This is the Triune God. Verse 4 concerns God the Spirit, verse 5 concerns God the Son, and verse 6 speaks of God the Father. Moreover, each Person is mentioned with some qualifications. With the Spirit, there are three points: one Body, one Spirit, and one hope. With the Son, there are also three points: one Lord, one faith, and one baptism. With the Father, there are also three points: over all, through all, and in us all.

THE DIVINE DISPENSING OF THE SPIRIT
AS THE ESSENCE OF THE BODY OF CHRIST

In Matthew 28:19 the Lord Jesus commissioned the disciples to go and disciple all the nations, baptizing them into the name of the Father and of the Son and of the Holy Spirit. In this verse the Father is mentioned first, then the Son, and the Spirit last. But in Ephesians 4:4-6, the order is reversed—the Spirit is mentioned first, then the Son, and the Father last. At the beginning, when we baptize people into the Triune God, the Father is first, because the Father is the source. Through baptism, people are baptized into the Body of Christ. The Body of Christ does not begin with the Father, but with the Spirit. When we are baptized, we are baptized into the Father, the Son, and the Spirit. Now in the Body of Christ, we are experiencing the Spirit, the Son, and the Father. In one case the order runs from top to bottom unto the result.

In the other case the order runs from bottom to top unto the source. Today, the church as the Body of Christ is in the Holy Spirit. If we are not in the Holy Spirit, there is no church. The church is in the Holy Spirit. Only when we are in the Holy Spirit can we be free from the flesh, and only then is there the church.

Ephesians 4:4 says, "One Body and one Spirit." This Spirit is the essence of the Body of Christ. An essence is more intrinsic than an element. The Spirit is not the element of the Body, but the essence of the Body. If we do not have the Spirit within us, we are not the church. We are the church because we have the Spirit within us. The totality of the Spirit in you, in me, and in all the believers is the church.

The divine dispensing of the Spirit as the essence of the Body of Christ produces a glorious hope in all the members of the Body of Christ, and this hope is that our bodies will be redeemed, that is, glorified (Rom. 8:23-25). Our whole being will enter into the divine glory. At present, our bodies have not yet entered into glory. But we have the hope that one day, when the Lord comes, our body of the old creation will be brought into the glory of the new creation. In other words, the Spirit within us is constantly sealing us, nourishing us, and saturating us. When He has fully saturated us, we will be glorified. At that time our hope will become a reality. Our body will no longer be a body of flesh; it will be a spiritual body that is permeated with the Spirit.

THE DIVINE DISPENSING OF THE LORD
AS THE ELEMENT OF HIS BODY

Ephesians 4:5 says, "One Lord, one faith, one baptism." This reveals that the divine dispensing of the Lord as the element of His Body causes all His members to have a life-union with Him in His divine element through faith, and to have a separating transfer out of Adam and the Adamic world through baptism.

The Lord Jesus is the element that constitutes us to be the Body of Christ. This constituting is carried out first by faith. At one time we had nothing to do with Christ. But one day we heard the gospel, and faith was produced in us. By this faith we believed in the Lord and entered into a life-union with Him. This faith caused us to be joined to the Lord and to His Body, the church. Furthermore, before we believed in the Lord, we were in Adam. By faith, we were transferred from Adam into Christ, but our relationship with Adam was not yet completely severed. Therefore, we needed baptism. Faith brings us into a life-union with the Lord, and baptism terminates our relationship with Adam.

Through one faith and one baptism, we have been joined to Christ and to His Body, the church. In this way, Christ becomes our life, and the church becomes our living. Before we believed in the Lord, we were in the world. By faith, and through baptism, we are joined to Christ and His Body. Through this, our relationship with Adam is terminated, and we are separated from the world. After being joined to the Body, the church life becomes our "world." If we are not free from Adam, we cannot be free from the world. Adam is the head of the world, just as Christ is the Head of the church. But now, we have believed and are baptized into Christ, and have entered into the church life because the church is the Body of Christ. At the same time, we are separated from Adam and the world of Adam.

Hence, Christ is the element of the church. With Him there is faith and baptism. Through faith, we are joined to Him and to His Body, and today His Body has become our spiritual world. Through baptism we are transferred out of Adam and are separated from Adam and also from Adam's world. Now the church is in Christ, being in union with Him and with His element, and being transferred out of Adam and Adam's world.

THE DIVINE DISPENSING OF GOD THE FATHER TO THE BODY OF CHRIST IN HIS BEING OVER ALL, THROUGH ALL, AND IN US ALL

After we have seen the divine dispensing of the Spirit and the Son to the Body of Christ, we come to the divine dispensing of God the Father. Ephesians 4:6 shows us that the divine dispensing of God the Father to the Body of Christ in His being over all, as the Father's overshadowing, in His being through all, as the Son's care and concern, and in His being in all, as the Spirit's presence, enables all the members of the Body of Christ to experience the Triune God and enjoy His rich presence.

The Father is both our God and our Father. His being our Father means that we are born of Him. His being our God means that we were created by Him. If we were only created by God but not begotten of Him, we are not in the church. By being born of God we enter into a life relationship and an organic union with Him. First, God created us, and then He begot us. Since we are created by God and born of God, our relationship with Him is twofold. First, we are God's creatures, and He is our Creator. Then, we are God's children, and He is our Father. If there were no children of God, there would be no church. We in the church have been both created by God and born of God. Thus, we are created as proper human beings and born as children of God. This is the church.

Hence, the essence of the church is the Spirit, the element of the church is Christ, and the source of the church is the Father. The Father who begot us is above us, as the Father's overshadowing. This is like an eagle overshadowing its young ones, and like a mother covering her children when danger comes. God the Father is also through us, as the Son's care and concern, and He is in us, as the Spirit's presence within us. Thus, the Father who is over us, through us, and in us is Himself the Father, the Son, and the Spirit—the Triune God.

What is the church? The church is one Body, one Spirit, one hope, one Lord, one faith, one baptism, one God and Father of all, who is over all and through all and in all—this is the church. In the universe there is nothing like the church. How wonderful it is! Ultimately, the church is a group of people who are in union with the Triune God and are mingled with the Triune God. The Triune God and the church are four-in-one. Because the Father, the Son, and the Spirit are all one with the Body of Christ, we may say that the Triune God is now the "four-in-one God." These four are the Father, the Son, the Spirit, and the Body. The Three of the Divine Trinity cannot be confused or separated, and the four-in-one also cannot be separated or confused. This mysterious union and mingling of the Triune God with the Body of Christ is for the purpose of dispensing. The Spirit as the essence of the Body of Christ continually dispenses Himself into us. At the same time, the Lord is constantly dispensing His element into us. Likewise, while the Father is over us, overshadowing us, while He is passing through us, caring for us, and while He is in us, remaining with us, He continually dispenses Himself into us. Thus, the church is the result of the dispensing of the Triune God.

When the Triune God dispenses Himself into His believers, the church as an organism is produced in the universe. Furthermore, the Triune God is continually, little by little, dispensing Himself into all the members as their element, their essence, and their enjoyment.

THE DIVINE DISPENSING OF THE HEAD, CHRIST, IN CONSTITUTING THE MANY GIFTS

Ephesians 4:4-6 speaks of the nature of the Triune God and what the church is. Following this, verse 7 speaks of the gifts. Then verses 8 through 16 reveal how the One who descended into Hades, who was raised, and who ascended to the heavens, that is, the resurrected and ascended Head, Christ, constituted His many gifts and made these gifts the gifts He gave to His Body through His divine dispensing. These gifts also perfect the saints through the divine dispensing that all the saints may be able to do the work of the New Testament ministry, which is the building up of the organic Body of Christ, so that all the members of the Body of Christ may grow up into the Head, Christ, in all things.

With verse 7 as an introduction, Paul begins to speak of the gifts constituted by the Head, Christ, in verse 8. After His death and resurrection, Christ in His ascension led captive those who had formerly been captured by Satan. In His resurrection and ascension, Christ not only subdued Satan, sin, and death, but brought with Him all those under Satan's captivity. In one sense, none of us has been to heaven yet. But in another sense, we have all been seated with Christ in heaven already.

When Christ resurrected and ascended to heaven, He brought us together with Him into heaven. There in heaven He presented us, His redeemed ones, as gifts to God the Father. According to Psalm 68:18, the Father gave us back to Christ as gifts. Not only so, Christ used the life that is in the Son to constitute all these gifts into useful people. Some He constituted into apostles, some into prophets, some into evangelists, and some into shepherds and teachers. All these gifted persons are able to speak and function by their speaking. God captured all those who were under the bondage of Satan, took them to heaven, and constituted them people who are able to speak for Him. God gave all these people to Christ, and then Christ gave them to the church (Eph. 4:8). This is the Head, Christ, in His ascension giving the gifts to the church.

The gifts whom Christ gave to His Body perfect the saints through the divine dispensing that all the saints may be able to do the work of the New Testament ministry. The gifted ones perfect and teach the saints just as professors in a teachers college teach their students. After four years, all those who graduate from a teachers college become teachers qualified to teach others. In the same way, after receiving the continual teaching of the apostles, prophets, evangelists, and shepherds and teachers, the saints in the church will all be perfected to do the work of the ministry, which is the building up of the Body of Christ.

On one hand, the gifted persons perfect us, and on the other hand, they dispense to us the divine riches. Their teaching is their dispensing, and our learning is our receiving of their dispensing. This dispensing and receiving cause the members of Christ to grow up into the Head, Christ, in all things (v. 15)—not only in big matters, but also in small matters such as the way we cut and comb our hair and the way we dress. In this divine dispensing the divine element enters into us and causes us to grow in life. As we grow, we are transformed. Our transformation issues from the inward dispensing of the divine elements hour by hour. The more we grow, the more we forsake the worldly and fleshly things, and are joined to Christ and His Body.

When we grow into the Head, out from the Head we will receive the dispensing of the rich supply. On one hand, through every joint of the rich supply, that is, through all the gifted ones, the Body will be joined closely together. On the other hand, through the operation in measure of each one part, that is, through every saint, the Body will be fitly knit together (Eph. 4:16). The joints of supply are like the frame of a building, which firmly fits the building together. In the Body the joints are fitted together in the Spirit to be the "frame" of the Body. Besides the joints as the frame, there are many other parts in the Body. Each part operates according to its measure, and this causes the Body to be knit together corporately. The Head gives the gifts to the Body, and the gifts perfect the saints so that the saints are able to do what the gifts do, which is the work of the New Testament ministry. In this way every part of the Body operates in its measure to supply the Body, and the Body will grow up and will build itself up in love.

(A message given by Brother Witness Lee in Petaling Jaya, Malaysia on November 5, 1990)

About the Author

Witness Lee was born in 1905 in northern China and raised in a Christian family. At age 19 he was fully captured for Christ and immediately consecrated himself to preach the gospel for the rest of his life. Early in his service, he met Watchman Nee, a renowned preacher, teacher, and writer. Witness Lee labored together with Watchman Nee under his direction. In 1934 Watchman Nee entrusted Witness Lee with the responsibility for his publication operation, called the Shanghai Gospel Bookroom.

Prior to the Communist takeover in 1949, Witness Lee was sent by Watchman Nee and his other co-workers to Taiwan to ensure that the things delivered to them by the Lord would not be lost. Watchman Nee instructed Witness Lee to continue the former's publishing operation abroad as the Taiwan Gospel Bookroom, which has been publicly recognized as the publisher of Watchman Nee's works outside China. Witness Lee's work in Taiwan manifested the Lord's abundant blessing. From a mere 350 believers, newly fled from the mainland, the churches in Taiwan grew to 20,000 in five years.

In 1962 Witness Lee felt led of the Lord to come to the United States, and he began to minister in Los Angeles. During his 35 years of service in the U.S., he ministered in weekly meetings and weekend conferences, delivering several thousand spoken messages. Much of his speaking has since been published as over 400 titles. Many of these have been translated into over fourteen languages. He gave his last public conference in February 1997 at the age of 91.

He leaves behind a prolific presentation of the truth in the Bible. His major work, *Life-study of the Bible*, comprises over 25,000 pages of commentary on every book of the Bible from the perspective of the believers' enjoyment and experience of God's divine life in Christ through the Holy Spirit. Witness Lee was the chief editor of a new translation of the New Testament into Chinese called the Recovery Version and directed the translation of the same into English. The Recovery Version also appears in a number of other languages. He provided an extensive body of footnotes, outlines, and spiritual cross references. A radio broadcast of his messages can be heard on Christian radio stations in the United States. In 1965 Witness Lee founded Living Stream Ministry, a non-profit corporation, located in Anaheim, California, which officially presents his and Watchman Nee's ministry.

Witness Lee's ministry emphasizes the experience of Christ as life and the practical oneness of the believers as the Body of Christ. Stressing the importance of attending to both these matters, he led the churches under his care to grow in Christian life and function. He was unbending in his conviction that God's goal is not narrow sectarianism but the Body of Christ. In time, believers began to meet simply as the church in their localities in response to this conviction. In recent years a number of new churches have been raised up in Russia and in many European countries.

OTHER BOOKS PUBLISHED BY
Living Stream Ministry

Titles by Witness Lee:

Titles by Watchman Nee:

Available at
Christian bookstores, or contact Living Stream Ministry
2431 W. La Palma Ave. • Anaheim, CA 92801
1-800-549-5164 • www.livingstream.com